Personalized Curriculum: Method and Design

O. W. KOPP
University of Nebraska

DAVID L. ZUFELT
Texas A and I University

CHARLES E. MERRILL PUBLISHING COMPANY
A Bell & Howell Company
Columbus, Ohio

International Standard Book Number: 0-675-09970-6

Library of Congress Catalog Card Number: 72-165115

1   2   3   4   5   6   7   8—76   75   74   73   72   71

Printed in the United States of America

Preface

The concept of universal public education may well be one of the United States' greatest contributions to the history of mankind. In spite of criticism, adversity, and even the present financial crises, the professional teachers of this nation have been successful in educating a generation able to land the first man on the moon. Furthermore, to a greater degree than its critics might believe, curriculum has moved in the direction of purposeful change. True, that which has been accomplished is only a prologue in terms of current societal needs, but classroom teachers are on the move; and there is more willingness to individualize, yes, and more willingness to personalize the curriculum than ever before in history. The challenge of individualization of program on a mass scale is staggering. Because this somewhat contradictory challenge must be met, this book addresses itself to the problem of personalizing the program for children. Our school personnel need support and help; they have already taken their share of abuse.

The passing of time has recorded man's continual change; the twentieth century in particular has witnessed so much social and technological revolution that change has become an accepted daily phenomonon. During this time, societal evolution together with sporadic social disorder has escalated education to a position of primary concern. Today acquisition of knowledge is synonymous with survival. Striving for excellence while educating the total population is the dilemma before educators in the closing decades of this century.

Within a global context, education encompasses new areas for study, including the extension of intellectual horizons to probe the unknown frontiers of inner and outer space, in addition to the omnipresent dynamics of local, state, national, and international living. In attempting to relate curriculum development to this stockpiled knowledge, a classroom teacher must adjust to technological change in which premium has been placed upon the utilization of programmed hardware, software, and the services of the computer. Both experienced and beginning teachers have been forced to come to grips with the problems of obsolescence as well as to wrestle with the assimilation of new substantive content, methodology, and innovative classroom management, techniques, and instructional materials.

The notion exists that schools assume a role of leadership which continually brings about significant change in social behavior. However, upon closer examination, school administrators and lay boards appear to react to external forces and follow the direction pointed out by pressure groups. For example, the launching of Sputnik demonstrated the contrast between a nation concerned with education as a service to the state and a nation concerned with education as a means of individual improvement. The Russian satellite triggered a chain of events which caused American curricula to be more critically evaluated and new programs to be developed. These developments have run their short-lived course, but serious curriculum design continues to make significant contributions to the learning experiences of American youth.

Personalized Curriculum: Method and Design describes curriculum development resulting from multifaceted involvement. At the local level, curriculum development has usually been a shoring up, fixing, updating of published plans or projects as they appear on the scene. This book emphasizes selected contributions of American educators who have affected contemporary educational thought. Forces affecting curricula are presented to illustrate the reasons elementary schools have adopted innovation and methodological changes in their courses of study. The book focuses upon guidance and the emerging role of the teacher. The guidance function is viewed as primarily classroom oriented, with a specialist available to implement and follow through on both fronts: child problems and professional in-service problems. Curriculum development is presented as a multilevel process which stresses the leadership expertise of local instruction, supervision, and administration.

Curriculum development within a format of individualized instruction is based upon an understanding of group dynamics and the teaching process. Therefore, the writers have provided the reader with guidelines which can be adapted within any local school organization. Inasmuch as successful curriculum development allows for faculty involvement and problem solving, implementation of preconceived curricula insures diminished acceptance. Invariably, where there has been a systematic analysis of need and faculty involvement, innovative change has been the result. In the final analysis, a teacher's attitude and self-confidence in his professional posture remain the fundamental factors in effective curriculum development and implementation. A society in continual change presents a never-ending challenge for educators to create curricula of lasting import.

A summary statement, major themes which highlight subject content, and selected bibliography conclude each chapter; flow charts and diagrams visually illustrate instructional models; sample forms and case studies relative to the guidance function complement the text.

Grateful appreciation is extended to Don E. Gribble, Chairman of Special Projects, UND, Ellendale Branch for his editorial assistance in the initial draft of the manuscript and to Sr. Camille Kenely, O. S. B., and Rex Hudson, Vice-president, College of St. Scholastica, Duluth, Minnesota, who graciously assisted in editing copy. The authors are also indebted to Marie O. McNeff for her contributions in the guidance area.

O. W. K.
D. L. Z.

DEDICATION

To those educators of children and teachers
who continue to seek ways of creating personalized curriculum experiences for each
learner.

Contents

Existence is a strange bargain.
Life owes us little; we owe it
everything. The only true happiness comes from squandering
ourselves for a purpose.

——*John Mason Brown*

1

A CENTURY OF CHANGE

OVERVIEW

Free and compulsory education may emerge as the United States' unique contribution to civilization. Elementary education, the fundamental element of this system, has evolved from bleak one-room rural schools into a broad base of comprehensive districts in both rural and urban communities. As elementary schools increased in number during the decades of industrial expansion, their political and social environment caused a variety of pressures to be exerted upon curriculum offerings, and in some cases, even affected the methods used by classroom teachers. Attacks on these schools and their curricula by malicious and uninformed critics, as well as by interest groups, were not uncommon. Occasionally specific suggestions, based upon research and field study, were offered as a basis for curriculum change and innovation; but more often than not, both method and curriculum design were determined by chance, fashion, bias, and crisis.

In the early period of public school development, emphasis centered on basic skills—the "Three R's"—because a majority of the population was illiterate. Later, as nationalism became the prevalent attitude, emphasis shifted to transmission of culture, with skills assuming less importance. More recently, and particularly since mid-century, a noticeable concern for the individual student's personal growth is apparent; however this emphasis is by no means nationally implemented or even accepted. Consequently, teacher inculcation of skills and cultural themes continues to be the dismal fare for regimented classes in many elementary schools across the nation.

Concurrent with these variations in emphasis, the economic progress of the nation induced its own changes in curriculum and method. When agriculture dominated the nation's economy, its requirements set the length of the school year at nine months, which is still the prevailing mode. After industry superseded agriculture as a dominant force, child labor laws were followed by compulsory school attendance laws. Demands from workers and the rise of unions brought an emphasis on training students for jobs in business, the trades, and industry. In the thirties, there was an increase in the number of science classes. But in most elementary schools, the newly developed technological aids available for use in the classroom went largely unnoticed or were ignored in curriculum construction and teaching methods. The eruptive changes technology was working upon society outside of the school were likewise unrecognized.

Around 1950, the nation awoke to the obsolescence of method and curriculum in its schools. Since that time, massive national efforts have aimed at reevaluating curricula and teaching methods so that the results of education would be in keeping with the life needs of students in their rapidly changing world. In such fluid and diversified conditions, a systematic assessment of educational effort can provide informative direction for method and curriculum policy at all levels of educational decision making.

Relying upon either rigidly prescribed or haphazardly constructed curricula, today's "lateral transmission of knowledge,"[1] therefore, would seem to deny an apparent truth of the technological age: "no one will live all his life in the world into which he was born, and no one will die in the world he worked in his maturity."[2]

Replacing the traditional teacher image persisting from an earlier and comparatively uncomplicated society, today's elementary educator-specialist now assumes a significant role in the academic, social, and spiritual development of children. Likewise, the curriculum has expanded from basic "Three R's" to include social studies, science, music, physical education, special remedial instruction, and programs for *exceptional children*.[3] It is here, in the elementary school, that behavioral attitudes, a creative spirit, and a life-long quest for learning begin to be formulated. Within the scope of a learning-living curriculum, a child's metal is

---

[1] Margaret Mead, "Redefinition of Education," in C. Scott Fletcher, ed., *Education for Public Responsibility* (New York: W. W. Norton Inc., 1961), p. 57. Lateral transmission is the sharing of knowledge by the informed with the uninformed regardless of age or academic preparation.

[2] *Ibid.*, p. 56.

[3] A glossary of specialized terms will be found on pages 127-30. These terms will be italicized at first usage in the text.

tempered, hopefully, to create a base upon which he can obtain a positive self-concept which will sustain him in his continuing search for self-fulfillment.

THE OSWEGO MOVEMENT

In the mid-nineteenth century, the learning theories of Johann Heinrich Pestalozzi became the basis for subsequent improvement in learning experiences which school provided for young children. As a "sense realist," Pestalozzi advocated utilizing objects that were selected and placed within the school environment to illustrate each idea introduced in any given lesson. Instruction took the learner from some point of knowledge to an inquiry about the unknown with the help of concrete illustrations. Incorporated into this sequence was the planned progression from visual objects to abstractions. Within this progression, learning experiences evolved from the simple to the complex and from the familiar to the unfamiliar. The Pestalozzian theory and method of instruction interested Edward Austin Sheldon, who established the Oswego Normal School at Oswego, New York, in 1861. Here prospective teachers of elementary school children were instructed in the application of the learning theories of Pestalozzi.[4]

As a pioneering effort to improve elementary education, Sheldon and his faculty exposed aspiring teachers of young children to the value of "field trips, shop work, and inductive lessons."[5] Here at the Normal School, "for the first time," elementary education majors became aware of "appropriate" classroom materials for children of different ages.[6] However, the antiquated method of reading and reciting continued to dominate classroom methodology. Beck et. al. state that the "object method" remained unchallenged for a generation.[7] After a bright beginning, the "object method" became a mechanical routine lacking systematic appraisal in terms of an increasingly more complicated society. Yet the inductive method has remained to be incorporated in new curriculum design and educational innovation today.

---

[4] Robert H. Beck, Walter H. Cook, and Nolan C. Kearney, *Curriculum in the Modern Elementary School*, 2nd. ed. (Englewood Cliffs, New Jersey: Prentice-Hall, Inc., 1961), p. 15: ". . . the assumption that learning is a process of generalizing upon a number of sensory experiences . . . and to insure that the desired generalizations are obtained, various sense impressions are afforded in a well organized sequence."

[5] *Ibid.*, p. 14.

[6] *Ibid.*, p. 15.

[7] *Loc. cit.*

The "inquiry" and "problem" solving approach, for example, have roots in such historical development as the "object method." Curriculum development has tended to be an evolutionary process—not revolutionary in orientation. Perhaps this, in part, accounts for the lack of clearly defined evidence of revolutionary curricula in the nation's schools. The tendency has been to identify curricula in philosophical terms with little or no change in design and implementation.

INTERRELATEDNESS—REALITY AS A LIVING PROCESS

Alfred North Whitehead provided educational philosophy with principles of learning which apply at all levels of educational endeavour. As one who did not believe in restricting experience, he feared that one day "creative intelligence" would gravitate to unchallenged ideas.[8] Whitehead describes this "educational freeze" as . . . "This is the correct thing to know, passive acceptance of polite learning, without any intention of doing anything about it."[9]

In the process of learning, feelings are fundamental to an experience which is interpreted in some aspect of a value judgment. Thus, in the conceptual years of the elementary school, a child's sensory experiences must be dealt with so that he perceives them as being manageable.[10] Sense experiences and an individual's feelings about those experiences affect the quality and quantity of stored human knowledge.[11] Hence, Whitehead alerts the classroom teacher to an increasing awareness of deficiencies in information presented to the learner. "Once learning solidifies, all is over with."[12]

Assuming that experience in learning should be broadly based and interpreted through many conceptual relationships, the interrelatedness of learning may not be dismissed lightly. It would follow that learning

---

[8] H. B. Van Wesep, *Seven Sages: The Story of American Philosophy* (New York: Longmans, Green, and Co., 1960), p. 368. "We must appeal to evidence relating to every variety of occasion. Nothing can be omitted, experience drunk, experience sober, experience sleeping and experience waking, experience drowsy and experience wide-awake, experience self-conscious and self-forgetful, experience intellectual and experience physical, experience religious and experience sceptical, experience anxious and experience carefree, experience anticipatory and experience retrospective, experience happy, and experience grieving, experience in the light and experience in the dark, experience normal and experience abnormal."

[9] Lucien Price, *Dialogues of Alfred North Whitehead* (Boston: Little, Brown, and Company, 1954), p. 63.

[10] Van Wesep, *op. cit.*, p. 413.

[11] *Ibid.*, p. 398.

[12] Price, *op. cit.*, p. 63.

which is fragmented and disassociated from reality is ineffective. Therefore, more attention should be given to the types of behavior that individual experiences evoke in the learner. Herein lies the value of the "spacious present" which Whitehad refers to as a "definite duration of time which hinges the past with the present."[13] Within this time, an individual's interrelated experiences develop levels of his "self-creativity," which is the "deepest and most universal process in the world."[14]

The sum total of individuals seeking "self-creativity," which is "essentially a self-organizing activity," culminates in the interrelatedness of man and his social experience. This social activity is fundamental to society. "Without adventure, civilization is in full decay. Creativity stops with satire . . . When freshness is gone, it is time to turn to something new."[15] So it is in principle for all dynamic situations: the interrelated creative adventure is vital to the life-giving experiences of elementary school children, who acquire feelings that germinate into attitudes, beginning transferable behavior.

LEARNING AS AN INTERCULTURAL ATTITUDE

Learning has been defined as a sum total of an individual's interrelated sensory experience. But despite the importance of continuing sensitization, William Heard Kilpatrick reminds the educator that man's survival depends upon his increased skill in human relations. Therefore, concern for "intergroup relations in a classroom, teacher attitudes, and instruction which will foster original, creative, and critical thinking must be a part of the education of youth."[16] Kilpatrick called attention to the school's duty within a rapidly changing society to assist in the development of responsible citizens who can create a new social order that comprehends the value to be derived from interdependent activities in a pluralistic society.[17] As a "social progressivist," he envisioned the need, in our times, for intercultural attitudes in which education would have to be a major thrust to effect change. Therefore, it would seem to follow that intercultural stability is fundamental to an emerging new social order.

As people have been forced to live closer and closer together in the technological age of the twentieth century, an omnipresent concern for self has become manifest. Since the individual's self-concept is

---

13 Van Wesep, op. cit., p. 424.
14 Ibid., p. 420.
15 Ibid., p. 432.
16 Beck et. al., op. cit., p. 27.
17 Ibid., p. 26.

created in association with others, an intercultural orientation to living becomes necessary. Without intercultural understanding, discrimination in many forms may emerge to "deny democracy, ethics, and religion."[18] Kilpatrick believed that an emphasis upon human relations through education could eliminate learned biases and discrimination.[19] In our times, indeed throughout recorded history, learned biases and discrimination have been sources of social conflict. This conflict erupted to engulf the whole world during the first half of the present century.

Thirty or more years ago, the goals which Kilpatrick set for intercultural attitudes may have seemed utopian to the great mass of classroom teachers. Yet the beginnings of a practical system were there.[20] Television and improved transportation can now bring the activities of people in remote places into the classroom for study. Video-tapes provide eye witness to history, thus recording primary experiences for analysis: one need not be starving to understand starvation and its social implications. In an earlier day, curriculum and methodology did not provide realistic study of living experiences which then could be translated into positive observable behavior.

Kilpatrick was ahead of his times and the rest of the nation in the search for attitudes oriented towards intercultural living. He drew a sharp distinction between learning about and learning to do. Quoting Guthrie, he said, "A student does not learn what was in a lecture or in a book. He learned only what the lecture caused him to do . . . It is essential that the student be led to do what is to be learned . . . We learn what we do."[21] Ostensibly, the learner responds to that which can be translated into life situations.[22] Thus, classroom teachers are challenged to break from training the mind per se. Instead, they are urged to involve pupils in living-learning situations involving others as a substitute for the read, recite, and examine regimen which is void of shared living experiences.

---

[18] William Heard Kilpatrick and William Van Til, eds., *Intercultural Attitudes in the Making: Parents, Youth Leaders and Teachers at Work* (New York: Harper and Brothers, 1947), p. 2.

[19] *Ibid.*, p. 44. "It is an effort to bring to bear as constructively as possible on actual and possible intercultural tensions and on the evils of all bias, prejudice, and discrimination against minority groups. In short, the efforts' of intercultural education is to remove and cure the bias and prejudice of such discrimination."

[20] *Ibid.*, p. 5–7.

[21] *Ibid.*, p. 8.

[22] *Ibid.*, pp. 10–12. Basic principles of learning that Kilpatrick considered fundamental are: "1. We learn our responses and all our responses. 2. We learn each response as we accept it to use as we accept it to live by. 3. If one is to learn anything as a thought or feeling or an act, he must respond with that thinking to some actual situation. 4. We learn each response in the degree we live it. 5. We learn each response, especially a thought or mental image, in the degree that we have a ready mental scheme in which to fit it."

EXCELLENCE IN REALITY

In a society of pluralistic values with a governmental structure like that of the United States, change lags behind knowledge. Even in critical times, positive change may be slowed for long periods of time. Education, one of the legal responsibilities of the state, frequently suffers static periods in reflecting change whenever the pressures of government shift the emphasis to responsibilities other than education.

The period between 1930 and 1955, even though a period of economic depression and war, saw the evolution of the concept of human development and child study. During this era the focus was placed squarely on the child. Perhaps the social and economic forces of the times were such that implementation of those concepts tended to be limited. With the advent of the post-World War II era, the evolving needs of society have been such that education has become the "great growth stock." Men of national and international stature—men like James B. Conant— helped attract attention to the rapidly emerging role of education with the intent of meeting needs of people from birth until death.

Educational reform, in one direction aimed at offering equal educational opportunity to all citizens. With continual international and domestic unrest, a strong emphasis on egalitarianism grew with it, creating the dilemma of equality vs. excellence. John W. Gardner poses the question for everyone concerned with education: "Can we be equal and excellent too?"[23]

An affirmative answer to Gardner's query requires redefinition of equality and excellence. Educational equality has been frequently defined as equality of opportunity for all those who have ability and seek self-fulfillment. Excellence, on the other hand, without benefit of legal definition, requires new understanding if it is to blend with legal equality. The old concept of excellence, indicating the elite of an academic group, has only limited application because it creates an ever-widening inequality.

Excellence in its current application emphasizes the individual who desires knowledge and is motivated to achieve that goal. It is the attitude of wanting to aspire to the level of greatest satisfaction in all human occupational and personal activity. Thus, by inference, an egalitarian and excellent society would evolve when its educational opportunities are available to each of its citizens according to ability and self-motivation, and when purposeful attention to individual differences enables each citizen to realize excellence of self.

---

[23] John W. Gardner, *Excellence* (New York: Harper and Row, Publishers, 1961), p. 75.

One recent characteristic of curriculum development throughout the nation is the special attention given to providing experiences that nourish diversified talent with which to maintain a vital and vibrant society. Those concerned with quality programming have made specific provision to allow for active individual participation, a prerequisite to "excellence." Even though the individual learner has become the primary focus in the learning process, "the achievement of self-fulfillment is difficult when one must face up to the fact that our society, at times, does not find it easy to applaud superior individuals."[24] But when excellence is perceived as a "toning up, . . . many more can try to achieve it than do. And the society is bettered not only by those who achieve it, but by those who are trying."[25] Thus, such developments as behavior modification techniques and the contributions of Skinner and Glasser are relevant because the outcome can be more individuals who are "toning-up."

Consequently, excellence in our times can be achieved when individuals believe and live two fundamental concepts, "a pluralistic approach to values and a universally honored philosophy of individual fulfillment."[26] Finally, free societies must work continually to prove their capacity to achieve excellence. In such a society, individuals who seek self-fulfillment work for a belief rather than exist in "pampered idleness."[27]

SUMMARY

There is an urgent need, backed up by social philosophy for continued appraisal of methodology and curriculum design in education. Therefore, curriculum that effects acceptable social change results from consistent analysis of social evolution by those persons who can, in turn, infuse those demands into life-learning experiences within public and private schools throughout the nation.

Major Themes

1. In a century where change is an accepted phenomenon, educators have had a difficult time adjusting to the demands of society in terms of curriculum development.

2. The object method, practical as it was, progressively decreased in effectiveness because life-oriented inductive lessons became mechani-

---

[24] *Ibid.*, p. 73.
[25] *Ibid.*, p. 133.
[26] *Ibid.*, p. 134.
[27] *Ibid.*, p. 148.

cal procedures, as they tended to become lost in a more complicated and demanding society.

3. An interrelatedness of sense experiences maximizes the quantity of knowledge an individual chooses to retain.

4. Intercultural attitudes are fundamental to a stable pluralistic society which seeks to eradicate bias and discrimination.

5. Excellence is a dynamic attitude and a way of life which causes individuals to strive for the highest levels of human activity.

SUPPLEMENTARY READINGS

Bereday, George A. and Luigi Volpicelle, eds., *Public Education in America: A New Interpretation of Purpose and Practice* (New York: Harper and Brothers, 1958).

Blau, Peter M., *Bureaucracy in Modern Society* (New York: Random House, Inc., 1956).

Burns, R. W. and G. D. Brooks, eds., "Designing Curriculum in a Changing Society," *Educational Technology*, Vol. 10 (April, 1970), pp. 7–57.

Callahan, Raymond E., *An Introduction to Education in American Society*, 2nd. ed. (New York: Alfred A. Knopf, Inc., 1961).

Coleman, James S., *et. al.*, *Equality of Educational Opportunity*, U.S. Department of Health, Education, and Welfare, Office of Education (OE 38001), Washington, D.C., 1966.

Conant, James B., *Education and Liberty: The Role of Schools in a Modern Democracy* (Cambridge, Mass.: Harvard University Press, 1953).

_____ *Education in a Divided World: The Function of the Public School in Our Unique Society* (Cambridge, Mass.: Harvard University Press, 1948).

Dearborn, Ned Harland, *The Oswego Movement in American Education* (New York: Teachers College, Columbia University, 1925).

Fantini, M. D., "Schools for the Seventies: Institutional Reform," *Today's Education*, Vol. 59 (April, 1970), pp. 43–44.

Kelly, Earl C., *Education for What is Real* (New York: Harper and Brothers, 1947), Chapter 2, "Some Assumptions in Education."

May, Rollo, *Man's Search for Himself* (New York: W. W. Norton and Co., 1953).

Nixon, R. M., "Message on Education Reform," *American Education*, Vol. 6 (April, 1970), pp. 30–34.

Rippa, S. Alexander, ed., *Educational Ideas in America—A Documentary History* (New York: David Mc Kay and Co., Inc., 1969).

Tenenbaum, Samuel, *William Heard Kilpatrick, Trail Blazer in Education* (New York: Harper & Row, Publishers, 1951).

Whitehead, Alfred North, *Adventure of Ideas* (New York: The Macmillan Company, 1933).

——— *The Aims of Education* (New York: The Macmillan Company, 1929).

2

FORCES AFFECTING
ELEMENTARY EDUCATION

RURAL AND URBAN AMERICA

Megalopolitan sprawl has spread over yesterday's pastoral communities. Discrete strip cities characterize the demographic conglomerate, where over four-fifths of the nation's people live.[1] In contrast, the *small town* as an independent economic unit has almost become history[2] because "the country boy never went back to the farm."[3] Nearly ten years ago, Taeuber stated that in Iowa, Missouri, and Nebraska, one-fifth of the people living in small towns were already at retirement age.[4]

How could this have happened? What forces caused millions of people to scatter across the nation and become metropolarized? Jones identifies plausible elements which have coalesced to escalate urban growth by siphoning off large number of rural youth and adult workers: "Henry Ford and the paved road made it possible for the farmer to shop in the county seat, if not in the metropolis." In addition, "the Hereford bull took marginal land out of crops into grazing land. Contract harvesting made possible the corporate farm where the empty houses warp in the sunshine and man watches the wheat grow."[5]

---

[1] U.S. Department of Commerce, Bureau of the Census, *Standard Metropolitan Statistical Area 1960*, Washington, D.C., 1961, as cited in "Sprawling Strip Cities, They're All Over U. S.," *U. S. News and World Report*, Vol. LI (Special Report: September 18, 1961), pp. 74–75.

[2] Dwight A. Neswith, "The Small Town," *A Place to Live, The Yearbook of Agriculture* (Washington, D.C.: Department of Agriculture, 1963), p. 179.

[3] Jenkins Lloyd Jones, "The Deserted Village," *The Tulsa Tribune*, February 6, 1965, p. 20.

[4] *Ibid.*

[5] *Loc. cit.*

Settlement patterns in Nebraska, for example, serve to illustrate a thirty-five year national trend of rural counties losing population to urban communities adjacent to main transportation arteries.[6] A "good" town has to have three basic elements: (1) good schools, (2) reasonable medical supplies and services, and (3) enough job opportunities to keep bright and gifted youth from leaving upon graduation from high school.[7] Today's small town does not have the drawing power of an urbanized society which guarantees continued growth for cities of 50,000 or more.[8] Therefore, megalopolis has become the dominant settlement pattern in the United States during the closing decades of this century.

With their marked concentration of people, urban belts continue to dwarf rural areas in the leadership struggles for the "lion's share of wealth, people, industry, and trade."[9] National escalation toward an overpowering urban-oriented society continues to accentuate the socio-economic disparity among and within geographic regions. The degree of disparity in turn conditions the amount and kind of support for public and private education. For example, children who happen to live in poorly organized school districts lack opportunity for education equal to that provided for children living in more affluent communities.[10] Thus, ". . . the times call for the broadest of training to increase flexibility and adaptability in a changing job world."[11]

In the face of the omnibus challenge to strive for excellence and educate on a mass scale, selecting what is to be included in a curriculum looms as a formidable task, especially in the natural sciences, where knowledge is stockpiling faster than it can be assimilated into the present curricula.[12] In adjusting to the ephemeral content of current curricula, educator–planners are often caught up in a "crisis syndrome." Bowles points out "that today's crisis will be tomorrow's routine, and that only modifiable facilities can begin to cope with the changes of emphasis the public expects."[13] At both the urban and rural ends of

---

[6] David L. Zufelt, *The Influence of Demographic Characteristics Upon Site Selection and Program Development in a Geographic Area* (Ed.D. dissertation, Ann Arbor, Michigan: University Microfilms, 1967), p. 6.

[7] Jones, *op. cit.*, p. 20.

[8] *Ibid.*

[9] "Sprawling Cities, They're All Around U. S.," *U. S. News and World Report,* *op. cit.*, p. 78.

[10] Charles F. Faber, "The Size of a School District," *Phi Delta Kappan,* XLVIII: 1 (September, 1966), p. 34.

[11] "Our Changing Population," *National Education Association Research Bulletin,* No. 3 (October, 1961), p. 76.

[12] John I. Goodlad, "Changing Curriculum in America's Schools," *Saturday Review,* Vol. XLVI (November, 1963), p. 65.

[13] Harold W. Bowles, *Step by Step to Better School Facilities* (New York: Holt, Rinehart, & Winston, Inc., 1965), p. 271.

the spectrum, the crisis syndrome has caused educational leaders to reflect seriously upon their responsibilities, both legal and moral.

PROFESSIONAL KNOWLEDGE AND MATERIALS EXPAND

At the same time the nation was becoming more urban, professional knowledge concerning human growth and development and learning and instructional materials was being developed. The works of Havighurst, Hurlock, Piaget, Cronbach, Snygg, Combs, Bruner, etc. provide insight into the nature of human growth and development and the learning process. This research has served as a basis for current curriculum development. Havighurst's "fundamental tasks" coupled with the knowledge of reasonable expectations for a child at a given age provide the student of elementary education with guidelines with which to develop realistic living-learning experiences within the total school setting.

The advent of increased professional knowledge was parallelled by the development of instructional toys, games, films, records, tapes, self-operating teaching machines, and programmed instruction. Instructional materials assist the elementary school teacher in creating learning experiences whereby children can become more active participants. Expanded professional knowledge of human growth and development, the learning process, and instructional materials has served to provide a basis for continuous refining, adapting, and designing of new curricula during the past decade—curricula which continue to be modified for continued dynamic education in the 1970's, as educators strive to individualize instruction and provide quality living-learning experiences on a mass scale.

HISTORY OF FEDERAL PARTICIPATION IN EDUCATION

Federal support of education is not a new activity. The government has actively supported education since the founding of the nation. The First Amendment to the Constitution states "Congress shall make no laws respecting an establishment of religion, or prohibiting the free exercise thereof." In addition, the "general welfare" clause of the Tenth Amendment allows Congress to enact such legislation as it considers necessary to the overall benefit of the nation, and the Fourteenth Amendment prohibits any state from making or enforcing any law "which shall abridge privileges or immunities of citizens of the United States." In fact, the First and Fourteenth Amendments to the United States Constitution have been used to guide the development of public and private education independently of each other. With the political expansion of the nation, legislators sought to insure free public education for the general populace; and in 1785, set aside by law the sixteenth section of each township expressly for supporting education (thereby laying the foundation for the nation's leading institutions of higher learning).

Congress established the United States Office of Education in 1876. Until the middle of the twentieth century, this department collected, analyzed, and disseminated data throughout the nation to initiate and stimulate the overall improvement of education.[14] Today, as a division of the newly created Department of Health, Education, and Welfare, the Office of Education has received the added authority to direct allocations of project funds—one part of the legislation enacted by Congress over the last fifteen years.

In the first two decades of this century, significant legislation provided federal funds for certain aspects of agricultural education. At the county level, the Smith-Lover Act of 1914 initiated extension service programs supervised by the county agent and also provided for professional education of agricultural and home economics specialists. In 1917, the Smith-Hughes Act provided grants to local school districts for initiating and/or improving curriculum in vocational agriculture.

Several decades passed before Congress enacted legislation to foster curriculum research on a national scale. By 1950, with international crisis again upon the nation, critics assailed the schools for not having personnel, methodology, and courses of study adequate to the educational needs of the nation. At mid-century, the National Science Foundation was formed to encourage evaluation of existing educational programs in the sciences. In 1954, the nation awoke to one of its domestic issues when the Supreme Court on May 17, 1954, ruled that segregation in the nation's public schools was unconstitutional. This historic decision influenced subsequent federal legislation.

National anxiety arising from the launching of the Soviet Sputnik jarred leadership into action. Reacting to this crisis, Congress provided substantial assistance for improvement of education for all American youth. The National Defense Act of 1958 enabled public school curriculum offerings to be evaluated; and, as a result, stimulated development of new curricula as well as revision of present courses of study. However, the most comprehensive legislation affecting curriculum planners was not enacted until 1963.

At that time the Vocational Education Act was enacted. It was designed to provide education for the underemployed and to rehabilitate

---

[14] Charles A. Quattlebaum, *Federal Education Activities and Issues Before Congress* (Washington, D.C., 1951), p. 8.

workers displaced by automation. The Job Corps aided children of low income families. Programs such as Head Start and the Office of Economic Opportunity Act of 1964 included enrichment and remedial instruction for the disadvantaged. During this same year, the National Defense Act of 1958 was extended, including a significant extension of the Civil Rights Act, Section 601 of Title VI, which states: "No person of the United States shall, on the basis of race, color, or national origin, be excluded from participation in, be denied the benefits of, or be subjected to discrimination under any program or activity receiving federal financial assistance."[15] This law specifically denies federal financial assistance to those public schools which practice discrimination.

In 1964, the Educational Policies Commission criticized Congress for not enacting general federal aid to education on a nation-wide level.[16] Congress passed two acts in 1965 which provided omnibus aid to education: the Elementary–Secondary Act and the Higher Education Act. These acts provided monies at all levels of educational endeavour, including funds for expansion of the state departments of education so that they might better provide quality service to local school districts. Yet although billions of dollars have been allocated in support of public education by the federal government, any change depends upon action by state and local leadership. Saylor and Alexander point out that "most influential" and "unchanging" forces operating upon curriculum planning are "extralegal" in orientation.[17] Consequently, even with a dramatic increase in federal appropriations to fund national programs in education, any tangible efforts at the grassroots of education must still await action for local administrators and lay boards in whom the Constitution and state laws have vested legal responsibility for directing educational policy and decision making.

EDUCATION IN AN AFFLUENT SOCIETY

Education in its broadest sense is now a function of survival and can no longer be considered a luxury for an elite. (See Figure 1.) Many of today's parents experienced the economic depression of the 1930's, participated actively in World War II and the Korean conflict, reared their

[15] 88th Congress, *Public Law* 88-352. H.R. 7152 (1964).

[16] Educational Policies Commission, *Educational Responsibilities of the Federal Government* (Washington, D.C.: National Education Association, 1964), p. 18, as cited in J. Galen Saylor and William M. Alexander, *Curriculum Planning for Modern Schools* (New York: Holt, Rinehart, & Winston, Inc., 1966), p. 28.

[17] Saylor and Alexander, *op. cit.*, pp. 28–36. Topics discussed include national curriculum projects, tradition, accreditation, colleges and universities, public opinion, testing programs, educational research, foundations and the education profession.

children in prosperity, and provided these same children with material benefits unknown during their own childhoods. As this younger generation comes to dominate the nation, its frame of reference is therefore one of economic affluence in consonance with the moral and sociological wrenching of a people wrestling with the struggle for civil rights and the nation's involvement in an unpopular international crisis.

Both parents and children have lived through the social upheaval of minority groups in urban communities and have witnessed revolutionary doctrinal change within their religious communities. Parents, conservative by age and experience, and youth, idealistic and active, seek avenues of ccmmunication leading toward better places to live and work. As the parents retire, the educated youth are continually frustrated because of the wide variety of available career choice. For the qualified, work opportunity is constantly diverse and continually multiplying, as are its demands upon leadership and human energy.

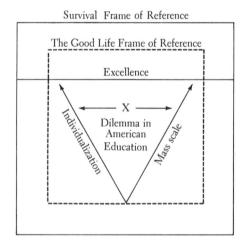

FIGURE 1

Survival Frame of Reference

Source: O. W. Kopp and M. E. McNeff, *Guidance Handbook for Personnel of Elementary Schools* (Lincoln, Nebr.: University of Nebraska Press, 1969), p. 5. Used by permission.

Education directly influences vocational selection and subsequent economic and social advantages, all necessary to the "good life." Thus, preparation for the "good life" also means the acquisition of knowledge for survival. (See Figure 1.) With free public education, a constitutional responsibility vested with the state, individualizing instruction on a mass scale creates a unique dilemma. (Again, see Figure 1.) In order to resolve this problem, change has to be initiated at the classroom level. However, since this change can only be effective when entrusted to competent professional educators, colleges and universities must respond by educating prospective teachers in an environment characterized by flexible planning, pupil involvement, individualized living-learning experiences, and innovative method and technology.

Teachers whose basic attitudes emphasize pupil-teacher relationships and develop the participation of the learner at his own level come closer to individualizing instruction on a mass scale. Prospective teachers who understand that quantity and quality of study performance and participation vary from and within areas of study, at all levels of learning, will be unlikely to resort to the dead-end learning situations in which pupil motivation and goals are only disguised teacher motivation and goals.

The graded, self-contained classroom under the direction of one teacher has dominated elementary education for over one hundred years. Only relatively recently, particularly since the thirties, have attempts been made to modify this "traditional" organizational format. Expanded professional knowledge has caused educators at the elementary school level to organize learning both psychologically and logically, where the learner becomes truly of first concern. When teacher-centered curricula directs learning experiences of children, the child is forced to assume the role of a passive learner. As a result, he may disrupt efficient classroom management. Observation of many school teachers seems to demonstrate time and again that eight to a dozen subjects—reading, arithmetic, science, English, history, geography, music, art, physical education, foreign language, composition, and penmanship—remain isolated and fragmented. Over time, we have come to equate this series of unrelated subjects with an acceptable comprehensive education. However, contemporary society's criteria of a comprehensive education and the individual learner's evaluation of it seem to be in conflict. Fortunately the contributions of the 1930–1955 period placing emphasis upon human development with greater stress upon the neighborhood school concept, child study, and more knowledge of the individual child were factors in the evolution of curriculum change. Herein lie the beginnings of an emerging emphasis upon a fundamental concept of guidance in the elementary school. The developments of this era, the thirties through the fifties, may well prove instrumental in slowly overcoming the problems of the teacher-centered curricula.

Upon interviewing hundreds of students from primary grades to the doctoral level and teachers or others who have reached retirement age, we have found consistently that the character of one or a small number of teachers excited the imagination of an individual in his youth, and made a difference for a lifetime. Conversely, some felt that they had been denied self-fulfillment because guidance and patience had not been a part of their living-learning experiences. Although older persons may have become specialists, their interest in their chosen field goes back to childhood; some teacher nurtured an insatiable curiosity from which evolved a life's work.

Adult success, apparently, often has its roots in the skillful guidance of elementary school teachers. Under their direction, learning explodes into a tumult of inspired search gathering momentum into adulthood. Despite the significance of elementary school experiences, the area specialist is seldom consulted and often overlooked in comprehensive curriculum planning. Too often curriculum design becomes a function of administration which neglects to include instructional know-how and information about learning abilities of individual pupils and specific elements within the school community which classroom teachers could contribute.

In the final analysis, a classroom teacher's attitude toward children and skill in democratic pupil management form the substance from which moral, ethical, and responsible citizens grow. Alex de Toqueville stated over a hundred years ago that "there is nothing more arduous than the apprenticeship for liberty."[18] This apprenticeship and individualization of instruction on a mass scale are basic to the philosophy of elementary education. At the elementary school level of living-learning experiences, intelligent guidance on an individual basis shapes emerging attitudes which one day will guide the nation.

Teachers in an Affluent Society

The world leadership and economic prosperity of the United States have brought material goods to a large proportion of the nation's people. Yet money has not been consistently appropriated to public and private education. There is often conflict between the district's effort and its ability to support comprehensive education for its youth. As a result, an atmosphere of militance pervades teacher contract negotiations. No longer are classroom teachers, especially recent entrants, willing to acquiesce to the dicta of administrators and lay boards of education. Professional unrest frequently inspires headlines such as "RECORD WAVE OF TEACHER STRIKES EXPECTED." Thus, in the last half of the past decade countless children in major metropolitan and

---

[18] Alex de Toqueville, *Democracy in America* (1840), Vol. I (New York: Alfred A. Knopf, Inc., 1951), p. 249.

rural school districts throughout the nation faced delays in opening the fall term.

The National Education Association and the American Federation of Teachers now represent most of the teachers and administrators at the negotiation table. Seldom is it realized or reported in the news media that higher salaries are not always the central issue behind teacher strikes. Thus, it is easily inferred that "extralegal" forces continue to affect the operation of elementary and secondary schools throughout the nation. Teachers are not the only persons who are interested in or who have expressed concern for the improvement of education. Conferences, seminars, and workshops continually meet throughout the nation, alerting those interested in educational improvement to the facts which classroom teachers and administrators face each working day.

Realizing that education continues to be the nation's number one growth stock, militant leaders have emerged in public protest via the strike and boycott, because teachers in some instances are asked to continue to undertake their professional assignment in conditions which were developed to function forty or more years ago—when the nation was agriculture–oriented. Our society has achieved an unparalleled standard of living. In this growth, the education profession has moved forward from dominance by lay boards and administrators to an increasing demand by teachers to share in the responsibility for policies that determine the present and future direction of the school systems. As a result of increased professional responsibility–sharing among teachers, administrators, and lay boards, cooperative, respectful, and systematic planning can bring increased educational opportunity to every school district in the nation.

The shared responsibility among teachers, administrators, and the private sector is of utmost importance when considering the increased educational opportunity. The 1960's were a decade when teachers, superintendents, principals, and parents tended to gravitate into opposing camps. The challenge of the seventies is to bring them back into an effective working relationship. Fortunately, as the seventies begin, the trend seems to be in the direction of teachers and administrators working together. Organizations such as the NEA lead in promoting increased cooperation between teachers and administrators. Teacher negotiations will not be diminished because teachers and administrators cooperate for the welfare of education. On the contrary, even greater teacher gains may be achieved in working out of a cooperative system. For, if the students benefit from a better living-learning experience, the dedicated professional will benefit as well.

SUMMARY

Despite the country's prosperity the United States has domestic issues to solve, where education and equality of opportunity are primary to national survival. Our cities and rural regions illustrate economic disparity and the ever-present need for improved leadership and funds to upgrade educational opportunity for all of the nation's youth. It is hoped that teachers and administrators throughout the country will join forces to demand a greater voice in shaping educational environments at the local district level, in anticipation of providing the best learning experiences currently available for the communities' children.

Major Themes

1. The United States is characterized by youth and an urban-oriented social order.

2. The federal government has supported and influenced selected aspects of education since the nation was founded.

3. Social disorder has greatly affected the scope and nature of the federal government support of education.

4. The dilemma in the United States today is how to individualize instruction on a mass scale.

5. The democratic classroom is a place where citizenship should develop and mature.

6. In the sixties, teachers have become more militant in their demands to share responsibility for directing educational policies and programs at the local district level.

7. From an apparent split between teachers and administrators in the past decade, some realization of the need for working from a cooperative frame of reference in the seventies is evident.

SUPPLEMENTARY READINGS

Bellamy, L. G., "Looking Backward: The Impact of Supreme Court Decisions on the American Educational System, 1969–1980," *Phi Delta Kappan*, Vol. 51 (February, 1970), pp. 313–15.

Doak, Dale, "Do Court Decisions Give Minority Rule?" *Phi Delta Kappan,* Vol. 44 (October, 1963), pp. 20–24.

Edington, D. D., "Disadvantaged Rural Youth," *Review of Educational Research,* Vol. 40 (February, 1970), pp. 69–85.

Galbraith, John Kenneth, *The Affluent Society* (Boston: Houghton Mifflin Company, 1958).

Green, T. F., "Schools and Communities: A Look Forward," *Harvard Education Review,* Vol. 39 (Spring, 1969), pp. 221–52.

Purcell, Francis P., and Maurie Hillson, "Current Issues and Findings Concerning the Disadvantaged Learner: His Education and His Life Chances," in Maurie Hillson, ed., *Education Current Issues and Research in Education* (New York: The Free Press, 1967), pp. 295–314.

Saylor, J. Galen, "Captive to Funded Projects," *Educational Leadership,* Vol. 26 (January, 1969), pp. 320–44.

Snow, Robert H., "Anxieties and Discontents in Teaching," *Phi Delta Kappan,* Vol. 44 (April, 1963), pp. 318–21.

3

THE ELEMENTARY SCHOOL—
ACCENT ON PERSONALIZED
INSTRUCTION

AN ATTITUDE TOWARD LEARNING

An Overview

Ever since man first yearned for knowledge, there were variations in the organizational groupings in which learning took place. At one time, tutors taught one pupil or a small group of children. In this setting, a one-to-one pupil-teacher relationship could be easily established. But as the need developed for educating large numbers of persons, both children and adults, other organizational patterns had to be developed to cope with increased numbers while still maintaining quality education.

With this as background, limited knowledge of the learning process, minimal facilities and teaching faculty, and professional leadership all have guided the American elementary school curriculum to its position today, where emphasis has reverted to intense concern for the individual and for living-learning experiences that provide a broad base on which to build positive contributing citizenship.

Evolution of the American Elementary School

From the time formal education became an accepted part of the total socializing experience of children, few formats included serious consideration of the anticipated characteristic behavioral and physical needs of children at specific age levels.[1] Curriculm at the elementary school

---

[1] Gladys Gardner Jenkins, Helen S. Schacter, and William W. Bauer, *These are Your Children*, 3rd ed. (Chicago: Scott, Foresman and Co., 1966), pp. 356–60. This work has a series of charts summarizing normal child development. The charts include the physical development, characteristic behavior, and physical needs of children ages five through adolescence.

level has been traditionally aligned with grade levels and ability group-ings based upon intelligence scores and reading ability. While many varieties of curriculum formats have been initiated within this century, even now many unfounded notions prevail concerning what, where, when, why, and how curriculum should be presented to the learner. These attitudes have been partly responsible for a rather stereotyped and rigid elementary school curriculum. The fixed, compartmentalized ap-proach to curriculum, still employed by many classroom teachers, has been shattered by studies such as those of Jerome Bruner. These studies support renewed experimentation, innovation, and adaptation in method and design, with particular attention given to the discovery approach to learning. Bruner states that "the hypothesis drawn from these studies is that if a child is able to approach learning as a task of discovering some-thing rather than 'learning about it,' he will tend to find a more per-sonally meaningful reward in his own competencies than he will find in the approval of others."[2] The attitudinal evolution from rigidity toward flexibility is graphically illustrated by a survey of the history of curricu-lum organization in the United States.

Pregraded Schools

With colonization and the American Revolution came a liberation from ignorance for everyone who sought self improvement. Although formal education had been provided by tutors for those children of affluent families, now children of those less financially able could study and enter the trades and skills as apprentices.[3] Prior to the Revolutionary War, education had been the province of the church and home. At that time, emphasis was placed on learning to read in order to comprehend religious teachings set forth in the Bible.

In the closing decades of the eighteenth century, popular textbooks such as *The Webster Speller*, *New England Primer*, and *Hornbook* were a primary tool of instruction in skill knowledge. Mass education did not as yet command widespread interest because schools had only been established in haphazard fashion, here and there. By the nineteenth century, education had come into sharper focus as the people and educational leaders such as Thomas Jefferson and Benjamin Franklin realized that mass education could preserve the new democratic form of government. The schools that then began educating the new citizens

---

[2] Jerome S. Bruner, "Structure in Learning," *NEA Journal*, Vol. LII (March, 1963), p. 27.

[3] Formal education refers to the traditional classical study undertaken by the socially elite of the time. While there were actual "schools" they were found only in the relatively heavily populated areas and were supported privately rather than by the government.

had a loosely structured, ungraded format, with continued heavy reliance upon primers, spellers, and the classical liberal arts.

Graded Schools

In the United States formal graded schools began with the Quincy Grammar School in 1848, where the chronological age of a child determined grade placement. Little or no consideration was given to the entrant's ability to learn and assimilate knowledge. Then, as now, many children experienced difficulty, and many of these students interpreted lack of success as unworthiness, which manifested itself ultimately in a negative concept of self. Research shows that children from homes from the middle and upper socioeconomic classes do succeed in the graded orientation; however, those children from deprived neighborhoods and limited experiencial backgrounds are and were at a decided disadvantage under this type of format.[4] Even now, graded schools dominate the nation's curriculum organizational pattern, some 125 years after a modest New England beginning. With its textbooks and tradition, this graded structure seems to have become an internship for middle class mediocrity, characterized by sameness and unchanging ritual where the individual is lost. The tenacious hold of the concept of the graded classroom on the community perception of education can only be changed by improved public relations on the part of those who are concerned with educational policy. Realistic change depends upon action by an informed and motivated public, by community leaders who realize that grade grouping is insignificant compared to the benefits of a continuous sequence of learning experiences under curricula which take into consideration the pupil's *developmental* needs.[5]

Self-Contained Classrooms

Essentially a concept of grades, a *self-contained classroom* is merely an extension of the Quincy Grammar School of 1848. Where the original graded classroom concentrated on the 3R's under the supervision of one teacher, the self-contained classroom of the modern elementary school includes responsibility for the expanded program which characterizes current school curricula.

Area specialists and consultants assist the classroom teacher in this particular modification of the graded school, now commonly accepted throughout the nation. One teacher may be working with thirty or more

---

[4] "Elementary School Organization, Purpose, Patterns, and Prospective," *National Elementary School Principal*, Vol. XLI (December, 1961), pp. 78–79.

[5] Ross L. Naegley and N. Doan Evans, *Handbook for Effective Curriculum Development* (Englewood Cliffs, N.J.: Prentice-Hall, Inc., 1967), p. 110.

pupils with area specialists in art, music, physical education, foreign language, and sometimes speech correction. Ideally, the classroom teacher and an area specialist work cooperatively to correlate the subject matter for the purpose of interrelated continuity—usually scheduled for specified periods of time each week.

Basic to the effectiveness of this system is flexible programming and the continuous association of one teacher with the same children in an environment where living-learning experiences can be created for both an individual and a group. Within this structure, a classroom teacher often has *auxiliary assistants* which assume activities formerly considered part of the teacher's responsibility. Even with auxiliary assistance and backstopping from community consultants as well as content area specialists, a single teacher in a self-contained classroom is responsible for directing the interrelatedness of the total curriculum for an assigned group of children throughout an entire school year.

The professional challenge of such an enterprise may exceed knowledge and energy limits of even the most able teacher. Its effectiveness varies adversely as teachers are less able. Thus, this type of organizational system does not necessarily make for anxiety-free transition from grade to grade. For instance, a child may have a less able teacher one year and a more able one the next; because a more able teacher may expect broader and deeper involvement than does the less able teacher, the child may encounter serious difficulty in fulfilling expectations—through no fault of his own. This traditional dilemma is a hallmark of the self-contained classroom. Pupils are unsuccessful because they are victims of circumstances, caught up in the administrative dilemma which pits their ability to learn against less and more able teachers. In spite of inherent instructional problems, however, flexibility and continuous pupil-teacher contact make it possible to implement a curriculum that consistently addresses itself to individual differences among a class of more than thirty children. Thus, all is not negative in the self-contained classroom. Perhaps "knowing" the children and assisting them individually offsets the teacher's lack of specialization in many subject areas. The question is debatable, but nevertheless, the self-contained classroom format is not totally adequate to meet the need of children in the seventies.

Heterogeneous Grouping Placed in the matrix of a graded self-contained classroom, several types of grouping have been initiated at the elementary school level. *Heterogeneous grouping* brings into one classroom a sampling of both social and academic situations together with students which cut across the school population in any community. As the school districts throughout the nation have experienced the pressure of increased population, grade levels have been expanded to more than one section. In this context, instructional strengths and difficulties in the graded self-contained classroom remain omnipresent. But a more striking phenomenon becomes apparent: heterogeneous grouping appears to be the safe approach to grouping for learning. Being sensitive to teacher and parental criticism of pupil placement and teaching assignments, administrators use this method of pupil disbursement to diminish greatly all forms of criticism.[6]

Heterogeneous grouping within a graded self-contained classroom places a unique demand for continual diagnosis upon the teacher. Basic instructional grouping at the beginning of the school year is professionally inadequate. When this grouping is allowed to solidify, the advantages of flexible programming and continuous pupil-teacher relationships are lost to structured unrelated exercises, ultimately sinking to the level of uninspired routine characteristic of another era. This heterogeneously organized classroom has diminished the availability of individualizing instruction in the self-contained classroom as it is currently managed. Experience shows that intraclass grouping created a tendency for the personal interaction of pupils to become subservient to academic performance criteria. Hence, all too often personal and academic development are conceived as two discrete entities. However, current knowledge of human growth and development and the learning process show that personal interaction and academic growth are in consonance with one another. The notion that schooling prepares one for adult living is but a half-truth. A child lives, he lives in his immediate experiences, and the success he achieves at this level directly affects future adult citizenship. Therefore, guaranteeing children the success they deserve in a graded, self-contained, heterogeneously grouped classroom depends on first reducing the teacher's pupil load to provide realistic instructional responsibilities. But reduction of class size alone will be of little consequence without insightful, continuous diagnostic evaluation and curriculum revision by the individual classroom teacher. Ultimately the empathetic, energetic, and dedicated professional becomes the prime influence in successful education of elementary school children.

Homogeneous Grouping   The concept of homogenity is, of course, a myth. However, within the graded self-contained classroom, *homogeneous grouping* has been a part of the elementary school. For several

---

[6] The building principal and/or school superintendent are still not insulated from extralegal pressures by teachers who feel that an assignment to a certain group of children is a reflection upon their teaching ability, and by parents who request that their child be placed with a specific teacher. Usually the parental request is based upon the comparative teaching abilities of teachers within a grade level and the parent's desire for his child to receive the best available instruction at the time.

decades, critics of heterogeneous grouping have championed this type of grouping. Often forgotten is the single fact that any functional program, regardless of its organization, only flourishes under stable leadership. The pros and cons are well known to the student of curriculum development. However, in spite of theoretical and applied strengths of this organizational pattern, mass public and professional acceptance are currently on the decline.

When an ability criteria becomes the determining factor for place-ment, a three or four track system is imminent. In our competitive so-ciety, parents are reluctant to have their children placed in the less-able grouping regardless of potential estimated ability or recorded perform-ance. In social status conscious communities where college is a criterion for acceptability, academic grouping is often approved by parents of rapid learners, but it seldom finds favor among parents of children of average or slow learning ability. Sharp and inflexible criteria for pupil placement immediately deny other individual differences and ignore the possibility that, at any given time, a child may relate better to one teacher than another.[7]

If guidance at the elementary school level is to be functional, place-ment based upon intelligence and reading ability must take into con-sideration other primary learning factors such as interest and aptitude, two elusive characteristics consistently neglected. The professional edu-cator has known for a long time that native intelligence and reading ability alone do not guarantee quality participation or performance in every area of study. Thus, despite reduced instructional range, unless regrouping for instruction is continuous, human growth patterns[8] emerge to create the traditional heterogeneous classroom.[9]

The primary level of the elementary school may be the easiest in which to use homogeneous grouping because of the emphasis placed upon the sequence of conceptual learning skills. In contrast, the inter-mediate grades begin in-depth study, where the curriculum tends to lend itself to departmentalization. In this situation, if reading ability becomes the major criterion for pupil assignment and if the curricula are not adjusted continually for individual differentiation, homogeneous

---

[7] Homogeneous curriculum organization often affects teacher morale—especially if a teacher has been continuously assigned to a slow section for several years. Few complaints arise from assignment to rapid learners. Many teachers who expound the need for considering individual differences among children do not accept this prin-ciple when applied to their own teaching ability.

[8] Jenkins, Schacter, and Bauer, *op. cit.*, pp. 356–60.

[9] Effective homogeneous grouping requires relatively large numbers of children. Therefore, most neighborhood elementary schools have difficulty implementing this concept because they have only 50 to 90 pupils per grade level. Rural areas with small constituencies have even fewer pupils.

grouping ceases to function well (if it actually ever did). Thus, in the graded school context, the over-all influence of homogeneous grouping upon curriculum organization continues to diminish.

DEVELOPMENTS IN CURRICULUM STRUCTURE

Middle School and Departmentalization

During the past decade the middle school has gained increased professional acceptance as an administrative unit. Educators now believe there is more similarity among children of ages 10 through 13 than among those of ages 5 through 13. This new administrative unit attempts to regroup children for better learning environments by departmentalizing. In the past, students first experienced departmentalized education when entering a junior high school. Today concern centers about the merits and disadvantages of departalizing curriculum beginning with ten year olds. Many professionals strenuously object to any type of departmentalization of the elementary school.[10] The elementary education specialist —a generalist with only a minor academic concentration—is concerned that the middle school may lead to a general departmentalization of the elementary school. Actually, it appears that the real reason for the existence of many middle schools is not developmental, but rather is a means to meet a building need within a district and to implement integration where that problem exists.

Proponents of departmentalization dominate the field of secondary education; elementary teachers are divided concerning its apparent merits as opposed to those of self-contained classroom organization. Some educators point out that departmentalization provides the students with a subject area specialist. However, regardless of whether the pupils pass from class to class or the teacher moves from room to room, the interrelated continuity so far deemed essential for elementary education becomes obscured. Furthermore, with such an orientation, children may have difficulty in identifying relationships between and among separate subjects. Another recognized disadvantage of departmentalization is that individual differences, a cardinal consideration at the elementary school level, may be overlooked because the subject area specialist has a total class load restricting him to a minimum pupil-teacher relationship—thought to be fundamental in the development of a positive self-concept. Too, continual adjustment to many and varied

---

[10] Departmentalization is dependent upon a subject matter specialist. In the past, this teacher has been concerned with her own major field and seldom understood her specialization's relationship to the total program.

educational situations through out a single day make it difficult for a teacher in the departmentalized situation to be acutely aware of the social, physical, emotional, and academic requirements of individual children.

When a departmentalized approach to living–learning experience planning operates at the elementary school level, courses may tend to be teacher-centered and adult-value oriented. Modifications such as the *semi-departmentalization* of curriculum have been designed in order to provide academic expertise while maintaining the atmosphere of the self-contained classroom. In one such arrangement, social studies and language arts including reading may be the responsibility of a home room teacher for one-half day. The remainder of the school day is divided into classes such as arithmetic, science, physical education, foreign languages, art and music, each taught by a subject matter specialist. Special classes—for example, art, music, and physical education—may not meet daily. Thus, semi-departmentalization of the elementary school combined with team teaching may serve as an acceptable compromise format.

Nongraded Classrooms

The first attempt to break from the graded classroom came with the concept of the nongraded school. Dean states that ". . . with the freeing of shackles and with the lifting of unimaginative mechanisms, we come to the realization that the true test of educational merit lies in its responsiveness to the range of human variability."[11] Thus, nongraded classrooms represent the first successful departure from traditional graded classrooms giving impetus to curriculum changes and subsequent improvement.

The nongraded classrooms, in theory, removes grade levels. A child is placed in a primary or intermediate unit where he competes only with himself, working within his own ability range. He is not subjected to standards of group performance, so failure in the instructional sense has been eliminated for him. Before, a child's failure to meet predetermined (and often inappropriate) standards often resulted in his acquiring a feeling of inadequacy. The nongraded school, accenting continuous progress, allows for the development of a more positive self-image in the beginning years of supervised study. Within this format, each child proceeds at his own rate which is continually subject to review and guidance by the classroom teacher. Because even a multitext approach may fall short of providing adequate experiences for children, effective nongraded programs use all of a local community as a living-learning

---

[11] Stuart Dean, "Nongraded Schools," *Education Briefs*, No. 1 (July, 1964), p. 16.

laboratory which is centered about the school's instructional media center, a key factor in successful programs. Because the program can be tailored to the child, anxiety about performance is less apt to develop. Thus, the nongraded elementary school provides an environment where a child becomes aware of his competencies through guided discovery in living-learning experiences.

Children have responded to this approach to curriculum, and their enthusiasm has carried over into the home. Anderson and Goodlad's survey found that where children had nongraded school experiences, their parents also supported that kind of organizational program.[12] In terms of meeting individual differences, the nongraded school that practices a continuous progress approach to learning remains the first departure from traditional classrooms that has been accepted by both the professional and lay community.

While nongradedness honestly attempts to individualize life-learning experiences for children, so-called "nongraded schools" may exist on paper and in curriculum guides, while the teaching faculty retains the attitudes and practices of graded classes. Nongradedness means the death of the controlling factor of many teachers' curricula, the textbook. Although individual differences may be provided for, continuous progress in such schools may be virtually nonexistent. Consequently, nongraded classrooms may become *ingraded classrooms*. In large elementary schools (more than 600 pupils), class grouping may have instructional levels which implement modified ability grouping based upon reading achievement. Even though this is in accord with the concept of nongraded classes, many classrooms within this format do not have sufficiently individualized teaching. When children are not consistently adjusted to learning situations in consonance with their demonstrated achievement, graded classrooms take over again. In sum, many nongraded schools have experienced limited success because of inadequate teaching facilities, limited community support, and a faculty that remained graded in practice.

Multigraded Classrooms

The *multigraded classroom* is not a new instructional phenomenon.[13] In the past, it took the form of the one-room school which had pupils ranging from grade one through eight or chronological ages from 5 through 14. This in itself is a minor departure from the traditionally

---

[12] Robert H. Anderson and John I. Goodlad, "Self-Appraisal in Nongraded Schools: A Survey of Findings and Perceptions," *Elementary School Journal*, Vol. 26 (February, 1962), pp. 261–69.

[13] J. H. Hill, "Multigraded Teaching," *The Nation's Schools*, Vol. LXII (July, 1958), pp. 33–38.

graded school. Even with its limitations, the one-room school provided an element of flexibility not present in many graded schools today.

Today's multigraded classrooms usually have a range of two or three chronological years. This grouping allows a child to work and play in a peer group similar to that of his own neighborhood. The flexible planning and individualized instruction of multigraded classes can be transitions for those traditional school systems desiring to develop nongraded elementary schools. This curriculum organization pattern allows the combination of a general specialist, subject area consultants, and team teaching. Multigraded classrooms may also be a viable setting within which "intercultural" attitudes can be fostered. In the familiar social atmosphere of the multiaged learning situation, children tend to achieve more success than they do in a graded structure.

Team Teaching and Cooperative Planning

Team teaching is a present-day instructional idea.[14] Along with cooperative planning among teachers, it attempts to bring special instructional knowledge and several teachers to a group of children. This arrangement has been implemented in both graded and nongraded classrooms in schools which practice continuous instruction—schools where providing more individualized instruction for each child remains the primary concern. Team teaching couched in continuous progress lends itself to flexible modular scheduling. With computer assistance, a child could receive a new schedule as frequently as once a day.

Effective interteacher relationships are essential to the functioning of this type of system; for, regardless of classroom organization, the team of teachers shares responsibility for the educational experiences of one group of children. Through cooperative planning and utilization of special professional preparation and teaching ability, each teacher assumes both major and minor roles in the instructional sequence. The team usually has a coordinator or head teacher, a member of the school's line staff administration, who assumes supervisory functions formerly carried out by the building principal or grade level supervisor. Often each member of the team specializes in one area of the curriculum while helping other members of the team in planning and instruction.

In schools that utilize this format, curriculum comes under continual review. As educators use case conferences for evaluating pupil change,

---

[14] Judson T. Shaplin and Henry F. Olds Jr., *Team Teaching* (New York: Harper & Row, Publishers, 1964), p. 15.

the child's social, emotional, academic, physical, and spiritual needs remain the primary concern. When a group of children are able to work with a given team for more than one year, they are likely to receive sequential learning experiences, enriching their education more than if they had to work with a new team each year. Team teaching and cooperative planning along with a continuous progress curriculum of education promise individualized excellence for many children.

Telling versus Lecture versus Inquiry and Involvement

Ever since teachers have been charged with the responsibility of working with children, they have shown a tendency to tell their pupils summarily what the teachers thought worthwhile to know. Consequently, in a *telling-lecture* situation, children have been forced to assume passive roles, either learning meaningless data or risking failure. When teachers are too concerned with content coverage, becoming slaves to the prescribed texts and workbooks, they find it increasingly easy to tell children important facts rather than allow them to discover principles and relationships by themselves.

Even though the educational importance of readiness, involvement, and transfer of learning are well known, children are still being forced to sit immobilized—hearing but only half-listening to what is being told to them. When curriculum is teacher-centered, adult standards, insights, and value systems pre-empt the child's concept of his world. The child's own view of his experiences, aspirations, and needs is seldom considered. Hence, pupil motivation is that of survival rather than curiosity. Grades become all important and learning is relegated, at best, to second place.

As college and university faculties inform prospective teachers about pupil–teacher relations and their effect upon pupil motivation for learning, children's interests, aptitudes, and skills are increasingly being taken into consideration when topics for study are chosen. When a pupil understands that he can make choices, that alternative approaches are acceptable, and that his ideas are of value to his teacher, an atmosphere of trust and creative action results.

Given the flexibility of an *inquiry-involvement* framework, a child can inquire about who, what, where, when, and why of a subject. In this framework, he seeks to discover ideas, principles, and relationships for himself. After a classroom teacher has acquired sufficient confidence in his own ability, he can then encourage and guide children in the systematic inquiry of problem solving, which is sometimes a very time consuming activity. Allowing children the right of inquiry and promoting their inner motivation is creative teaching. Thus, individual growth patterns are the central concern as educational experiences are being articulated for boys and girls in the elementary school.[15] Inquiry and genuine involvement make the acquisition of knowledge the primary concern for the learner. In such an environment, external standards become less important. School assumes a new status for many children who have experienced some self-fulfillment. School now represents personal success and emerging identity instead of anxiety and *traditional failure.*

Programmed Learning and Instructional Materials Center

Programmed learning is a recent innovation in education. As a sequential self-taught study, it has value at the concept and skill level for elementary school children. Programmed learning allows a pupil to be independent of his teacher and to utilize better the available instructional time. It has been used as a supplementary teaching device where large numbers of children are involved. Self-administered evaluation devices accompany the program. A rapid check identifies incorrect responses, and the pupil can evaluate his own limitations in each part of his study. Another advantage of programmed learning is its adaptability to any type of grouping, allowing individualized study. It can be used for remedial learning, enriched programs, and supplementary study with otherwise rigid formats of day to day study.

The *instructional media center* is also increasing its influence upon elementary school curricula. In this setting, pupils use filmstrips, projectors, recordings, record players, and tape recorders with the same ease as library books. A recent survey showed that teachers and administrators were making special efforts to utilize resource material more efficiently.[16] Loherer's progress report states that the instructional media center provides for a greater flexibility in utilization of materials and that there is an attitude of importance affixed to the media center's place in the curriculum.[17] This innovation has obtained enough professional stature that new school buildings are being designed around media centers as a primary vehicle of curriculum development. With this reservoir of material, curriculum planning has reached near optimum flexibility for individualizing instruction.

---

[15] Jenkins, Schacter, and Bauer, *op. cit.*, pp. 356–60.

[16] Alice Loherer, "School Libraries as Instructional Materials Centers with Implications for Training: A Progress Report of this Study Under Title VI, National Defense Education Act" (Washington, D.C.: U.S. Department of Health, Education, and Welfare, Office of Education, 1964), p. 14.

[17] *Loc. cit.*

Individualization of Instruction

Individualization of instruction, more than ever before, has become the focal point of the learning process. However, the education profession is challenged with coping with titanic numbers of children per classroom. Fortunately, the flexibility of the continuous progress organization for learning—utilizing team teaching, programmed instruction, instructional media centers, and supplementary and auxiliary personnel—produces a coordinated environment in which children can be educated individually on a mass scale. Within this framework, a child is not ridiculed and consistently works within the context of his own motivation under the guidance of a classroom teacher.

Critical to such an organization is programmed instruction, which can meet highly developed skill needs. The teacher then has time to plan more creative living-learning experiences with the pupils. Furthermore, the learner can be an active participant from the beginning planning through the evaluation of the unit of study. At no time does the child have to assume the passive role characteristic of the graded teacher-centered classroom. Other forms of grouping may be integrated within the concept of individualization. *Team learning*, for instance, may prove to be a valuable intragroup structure because children enjoy working together. In this grouping an individual has the opportunity to be involved in both transmission of knowledge and interrelatedness of educational experiences. Those people who tend not to trust pupils working in teams worry needlessly, because integrity is a premium peer-determined behavioral characteristic when children have been a part of the initial preplanning. This curriculum organization could be an intermediate step in a phase-in program of continuous progress within any school system. Although no panacea, individualization of instruction under the guidance of the empathetic professional elementary education specialist can make significant strides toward excellence in education on a mass scale.

A CHILD AS AN INDEPENDENT LEARNER

Child of the Contemporary Scene

Each year, the elementary school child returns to the classroom to participate in another ten month period of learning experiences. He is a product of "now"—without memory of past decades, but with a varied background. Large population centers, widespread travel, and television have combined to provide today's elementary school child with both primary and vicarious knowledge and experience unknown to the child of thirty years ago. Even among lower economic classes, the elementary school child may come from a home which is dominated by material goods and mass media. Today's six year old comes to his formal learning environment with more academic know-how and social awareness than the teen-ager of past decades had. At the same time, the contemporary child lives in a whirlwind of stress, activity, and decision which his teacher did not experience and often does not understand. Today, pressure for involvement in extracurricular activities causes many children to get caught up in a work day of directed study, social activity, and homework that may be longer than their parents' work days. The societal preoccupation with involvement and acceptance tends to disrupt young lives and create a myriad of emotional problems. To add to the stresses acting upon today's child, he finds himself in a classroom in transition. His teachers are adapting their new theoretical understanding of curriculum planning and problem diagnosis to the practical situation of the classroom.

All of these stimuli may mean that the child has grown up with little restraint and required self-discipline. His family life may lack the kind of consistent dynamics which foster and promote motivation to acquire knowledge as a means of self-improvement. Within any one classroom, there can be children who perceive their formal education in many different ways, ranging from acceptability to irrelevance. This latter attitude often comes from a child who finds structured curriculum difficult to comprehend and deal with; and who, as a result, capitulates in quiet desperation. This wide range of attitude cuts across all economic sectors of the populace—both urban and rural. As a result, both the potential for excellence and for dropouts are conceived and nurtured in the elementary school.

In our geographically mobile society, it is also significant that the physical settings of elementary schools vary widely—from the one-room school to centralized, consolidated districts to village centers to urban community schools. Most of these buildings have been organized to process groups of children. They contain a series of self-contained classrooms in which teachers transmit facts. Education functions as a separate community service in buildings designed for indestructibility rather than for life-learning situations.[18]

The child of twelve emerges as a learner whose quality of learning experiences is a result of circumstances. This same child bounces from grade to grade, taught by teachers who represent up to forty years'

---

[18] Harold B. Gore, "The School of Tomorrow—Ten Trends," in *The School of Tomorrow* (New York: Macfadden-Bartell Corporation, 1964), p. 20.

differences in professional preparation. In this environment today's elementary school child must wrestle toward learning independence. His plight is not a new one, but today he grapples with a more complex set of uncontrollable circumstances. As a result, the urgency of modifying curricula to provide for individualization becomes a tremendous effort which demands solution.

Self-Fulfillment and the Learning Environment

Fundamental to achieving independence as a learner is the student's "right to feel success in the classroom, regardless of . . . ability." Today, as at no other time, there is a mandate to provide those experiences that allow the individual the opportunity to find fulfillment. The education of elementary school children must increasingly become child-oriented, while subject matter per se must cease to reign. Mastery of skills should be primary only in so far as the skill may assist the child in becoming a more informed person capable of increased positive participation as a citizen.[19]

Unfortunately, extralegal forces may thwart these envisioned education advances. Since World War II spending, particularly by the government, has escalated in every facet of living; as a result, people are extremely cautious. The continual rejection of annual school budgets and the increased incidence of teacher strikes throughout the nation are symptomatic of these evolving attitudes. Conflicts over philosophy and the direction innovation should take pose a crucial problem. In addition, sweeping proposals at the state and national level encompassing large numbers of school districts often jeopardize curriculum reform, because effective curricula must be developed in terms of educational need at the local level, resulting from a systematic evaluation of educational goals and local potential in terms of effort and extralegal forces.

It is widely accepted that every child as an independent learner deserves the opportunity to be provided with an educational environment which guarantees him a series of articulated experiences that can foster his motivation to continue to learn for self-improvement. To this end, curriculum and school structure have changed drastically during the twentieth century. However, attitudes about instruction methods, both lay and professional, lag behind.

Leadership within the profession may itself serve as a force to diminish educational progress. Often, at all levels of the profession, when financ-

---

[19] O. W. Kopp and Marie O. McNeff, *Guidance Handbook for Personnel of Elementary Schools* (Lincoln, Nebr.: The University of Nebraska Press, 1969), pp. 7–9.

ing is inadequate, educators compromise with minor personal policy changes rather than fully analyzing the problem and improving the basic issues. In some cases, educators decide to do nothing, to be safe and protect the status quo. Handling issues with nonaction solves problems by default, allowing known issues and problems only to become further entrenched. Moreover, changes that are continually postponed become proportionately more difficult to institute with the passage of time. Remaining aloof from problems is thus a dangerous position for professional personnel to assume. At the same time, leadership has been criticized for treating the product of the school system rather than correcting what Fantini and Weinstein refer to as an "outdated process." In fact, they suggest that the nation has spent "its energies at the fringes," that

> All American children are educationally disadvantaged; despite the avalanche of educational activity and the surge of additional money we are still in the business of repairing an anachronistic machine; we are laboring to serve the needs of academic subjects, not the needs of children; there is less wrong with the learner (the product of education) than with the process and institutions by which he is taught; the school, no less than the hospital, should be the main arena for professional training and research as well as practice; good schools should be defined not by their racial composition but by the quality of what happens in the school . . .[20]

In order to assist the individual, federal programs have provided funds for old programs in a new format. Therefore, innovation and change for benefit of today's children has been negligible. Moreover, it would seem that participation in federal programming has been undertaken in some instances for the purpose of acquiring additional revenue per se, with little or no regard for improving or revitalizing curricula. For example, during the summer of 1970, an eleven member task force studied ways and means to make Title I (ESEA 65), the biggest and most controversial source of federal monies to the elementary and secondary schools, work more effectively. Title I funds were not always being spent for the purpose set out in the original legislation. Program implementation at the local level, which is under the direction of the federal government, apparently has not been without its problems.

---

[20] Mario D. Fantini and Gerald Weinstein, "Taking Advantage of the Disadvantaged," *The Record* (Teachers College, Columbia University) (November, 1967), p. 103.

Educators must keep in mind the opposing extralegal forces that serve to block advancement, thus keeping school organization and curriculum in a state of transition, in order to provide the individual learner with an acceptable environment which is continually being modified. The transitional school incorporates the innovations of technology, personnel grouping, methods, curriculum design, and flexibility. In the final analysis, an elementary school child's opportunity to become an independent learner with a positive self-image depends upon competent instruction, reasonable class size, adequate instructional materials (software–hardware), enlightened supervision, and an administration which cooperates with lay boards that are leadership-oriented.

MEDIA AND LEARNING EXPERIENCES

A Preoccupation with Text and Workbooks

Textbooks have reigned for nearly two hundred years as the primary instrument of instruction. This single repository of selected knowledge has been (in most instances) a restricting vehicle. Before the knowledge explosion of the past quarter-century, life was less complicated and we were more isolated from international events. The agrarian culture did not place the demands upon its citizens that the current urban society does. A text was then more acceptable in its place as the beginning and end of substantive inquiry.

In recent years, textbooks have been accompanied by workbooks which function as supplementary works. In this way a child could be kept busy while other group activity took place. Workbooks usually required short responses which tested accumulated data relative to instructed material. Seldom was a child requested to reflect and analyze problematic situations based upon the learned data. Thus, a text–workbook approach to learning tends to limit learning. Learning can be further restricted by its use as an instructional tool by the elementary school teacher, and can easily be regulated to routine in both the acquisition and evaluation of knowledge. Confinement to the text-workbook perimeter often diminishes and in time may extinguish an individual's inquisitive quest for knowledge.

Media: Use or Storage

While it is possible to become preoccupied with using varying media in the classroom, the recent developments in educational media nevertheless do offer real possibilities for individualizing learning. Classroom teachers use audio-visual media to varying degrees; however, the frequency of use has been minimal. Most materials have primarily been used for entertainment; movies, filmstrips, and records are rented or obtained from central supply. They often have to be ordered as far ahead as one school year, thus causing many teachers to omit unusual media from their preparations. Within the past decade, media (software–hardware) has glutted the educational scene. The classroom teacher may be unaware of the availability of materials or not know how to operate equipment, which then gets stored away—out of use. Instruction in the use of audio-visual equipment has been included in the sequence of teacher education only recently; this is not as yet a nationwide phenomenon. Too, the available media still are entertainment-oriented. Thus the question of use or storage is of real concern. When the classroom teacher feels adequate in the operation and instructional use of audio-visual media (software–hardware) and realizes its significant contribution to the learning process, this vast resource will be properly utilized and living–learning experiences for an individual child will be enriched.

Mandate for Action

Today the range of instructional proficiency of classroom teachers covers a wide spectrum from the teacher who uses only the text-workbook to the teacher who uses "self-teaching" audio-visual equipment, relegating himself to dispensing materials and equipment with intermittent evaluation. Neither of these extremes is acceptable. Multimedia's influence in the teaching-learning process is as effective as the individual teacher's genius at creativity in a flexible instructional format. Consistent use of films, filmstrips, single concept loops, tapes, slides, photographs, acetate frames, and *found stuff*—rocks, snakes, leaves, logs—by the classroom teacher and reliance upon them as learning tools by individual students can cause knowledge to explode in many dimensions. Each pupil, regardless of ability, can participate successfully in learning.

Each child has the right to experience success. Acceptance of individual differences on an academic level is no longer enough. Because audio-visual media are available, the classroom teacher is obligated to create multi-level living-learning experiences for *differential learning* abilities. In as much as the teacher remains a pivotal key to effective learning, it is he who must accept the responsibility for the quality of experience in a given classroom. The teacher who chooses to remain professionally static, refusing to include appropriate audio-visual dimensions in his instructional set, must come to grips with the fact that the children in his classroom may be learning in spite of their teacher rather than because of him.[21]

SUMMARY

In two centuries, education in the United States has moved from an elite tutorial system to one of equality of educational opportunity for the entire nation. Extralegal forces continue to create an educational lag; the quickening pace of curriculum organizational patterns and a variety of the graded classrooms still dominate the scene. In contrast, more promising aspects for the future can be seen by the emergence of a primary concern at the local level for individualized instruction through continuous progress, team teaching, and emphasis upon the importance of the role played by the instructional media center in curriculum planning and study. The overriding principle to remember is that no one curriculum organizational pattern will solve everyone's instructional problems. Diagnosing need and seeking the proper mix of organizational patterns to meet individual differentiation is the professional responsibility of enlightened leadership at the local school and district level.

Major Themes

1. The graded self-contained classroom characterized by text-workbook dominance and fixed schedules is still representative of the major curriculum organizational pattern throughout the United States today.

2. Continuous progress, team teaching, and instructional media centers appear to be elements of an instructional mix with which quality education could be provided on a mass scale at the elementary school level.

3. Educational innovation and change are effective as long as informed leadership and enthusiastic faculty remain stable.

---

21 John Holt, *How Children Fail* (New York: Dell Publishing Company Inc., 1964), p. 158. "We ask children to do for most of a day what few adults are able to do even for an hour. How many of us [who] attend a lecture that doesn't interest us, can keep our minds from wandering? . . . Yet children have far less awareness and control of their attention than we do. No use to shout at them to pay attention. If we want to get tough about it, as many schools do, we can terrorize a class of children into sitting still with their hands folded and their eyes glued on us, on somebody, but their minds will be far away."

4. Curriculum organizational patterns must be continually revised in order to keep pace with changing educational requirements of our technology oriented society.

5. Fundamental to achieving independence as a learner is the right to obtain success regardless of ability.

SUPPLEMENTARY READINGS

Anderson, D. Carl, "Open-plan Schools: Time for a Peek at Lady Godiva," *Education Canada*, Vol. 10 (June, 1970), pp. 2–6.

Anderson, R. H., "The Nongraded School: An Overview," *National Elementary Principal*, Vol. 47 (November, 1967), pp. 5–10.

Aspy, D. N., "Groping or Grouping for Teachability," *Contemporary Education*, Vol. 41 (May, 1970), pp. 306–10.

Barnickle, Donald W. and R. T. Landberg, "Team Approach is Essential in a Nongraded School," *Illinois Education*, Vol. 58 (May, 1970), pp. 385–86.

Blair, Medill, and Richard G. Woodward, *Team Teaching in Action* (Boston: Houghton Mifflin Company, 1964).

Bruner, Jerome S., "Structure in Learning," *NEA Journal*, Vol. LII (March, 1963), pp. 26–27.

Combs, Arthur W., "Fostering Self-Direction," *Education Leadership*, Vol. XXIII (February, 1966), pp. 373–76.

Deterline, W. A. (ed.), "Programmed Instruction Today," *Educational Technology*, Vol. 10 (July, 1970), pp. 29–47.

Franklin, M. P., "Multigrading in Elementary Education," *Childhood Education*, Vol. 43 (May, 1967), pp. 513–15.

Frost, Joe L. and G. Thomas Rowland, *Curricula for the Seventies—Early Childhood Through Early Adolescence* (Boston: Houghton Mifflin Company, 1969).

Housego, B. E. J., "Nongraded Elementary School: Selected Problems," *Canadian Education Research Digest*, Vol. 8 (September, 1968), pp. 245–56.

McLoughlin, W. P., "The Phantom Nongraded School," *Phi Delta Kappan*, Vol. 49 (January, 1968), pp. 248–50.

Miller, Jack W. and Haroldine G. Miller, "Individualizing Instruction Through Diagnosis and Evaluation," *Childhood Education,* Vol. 46 (May, 1970), pp. 417–21.

Miller, Richard I., *The Nongraded School: Analysis and Study* (New York: Harper and Row, Publishers, 1967).

Morrison, R. R., "Is Specialization the Answer?—The Departmental Classroom Revisited," *Elementary School Journal,* Vol. 68 (January, 1968), pp. 206–12.

National Education Association Research Division, Research Bulletin, *Ability Grouping: Summary,* Vol. 46 (October, 1968), pp. 74–76.

Shuster, Albert and Milton Ploghoft, *The Emerging Elementary Curriculum —Methods and Procedures,* 2nd ed. (Columbus, Ohio: Charles E. Merrill Publishing Company, 1970).

Skinner, B. F., *The Technology of Teaching* (New York: Appleton–Century–Crofts, 1968).

Strickland, Joann H. and William Alexander, "Seeking Continuity in Early and Middle School Education," *Elementary School Journal,* Vol. 68 (April, 1968), pp. 387–400.

Tyler, Ralph W., "The Curriculum Then and Now," *The Elementary School Journal,* Vol. LVII (April, 1957), pp. 364–74.

Wolfson, B. J., "Pupil and Teacher Roles in Individualized Instruction," *Elementary School Journal,* Vol. 68 (April, 1968), pp. 357–66.

4

CURRICULUM DEVELOPMENT— A RESPONSE TO CONTINUAL CHANGE

A TOTAL FACULTY FUNCTION

Philosophy and Educational Objectives

Curriculum development must be based on a valid philosophy of education that represents the functional base upon which motivation of the participants is guided. In effect, the educational philosophy of an individual or group is the operational attitude which permeates all activity. While verbalized and functional philosophies may not be the same, an expressed educational philosophy and the degree to which it is practiced from the onset of curriculum design delimit the parameters in which participants function.

At the initial stage of curriculum design, personal ambition with a desire for "empire building" may scuttle otherwise worthy innovation. Genuine sincere concern for the learner and his improvement must be constantly in focus and supercede personal reward. Those programs developed about strong personalities in key administrative roles who impose change without the involvement and the consent of the participants eventually erode because genuine concern for the learner was not articulated. Consistent interest in the individual learner is known to lead to successful, and thus permanent, innovation, providing for mutual professional confidence among the participants. At this point, once confidence has been earned and mutual respect established, change has a better chance of becoming reality.

Logically, a curriculum innovation must be couched in terms of the school's articulated educational objectives. Unfortunately, these objectives are all too often only nebulous phrases or intuitive agreements.

When educational objectives have been delineated, they are the professional educators' thinking of what is "best"; hopefully these include the parents' aspirations for their children. In addition, objectives should be statements in terms of *behavioral objectives*. These terminal educational objectives must be determined in advance of curriculum design because desired end pupil characteristics can shape the kind and quality of curriculum required. In the past, curriculum design and change have more often than not been initiated without determination of expected outcome. The curriculum design has thus been a less than deliberate sporadic series of experiences.

Effort Capability

Essential to curriculum design is an analysis of effort capability, the local school district's present and potential finances, physical plant, hardware/software, and professional-auxiliary personnel which can implement selected programs. Once the effort capability has been ascertained, the examination of its use is the next step to be taken systematically. Teacher effort is a crucial factor. When designing the curriculum every member of the faculty should not be involved, because each can not participate at the same level because of varying professional competence. Total involvement is a myth. To insist upon everyone on the faculty getting "into the act" before curriculum division begins may mean that to all intents and purposes the project will never get under way. Thus, curriculum design will become the responsibility of an elite core of the best qualified personnel for that particular project which will in turn obtain and utilize pertinent information from the faculty who function as resource persons. Final adoption of the program then becomes a "total" faculty function.

Often relegated to last concern are the physical plant, hardware, software, and finances necessary to maintain and obtain additional facilities including additional faculty and auxiliary personnel. Because these factors have been relegated to being final considerations rather than being continuous referral points, many programs involving thousands of dollars of contributed service by faculties and hired consultants have been rejected. After the initial demanding involvement by school faculty members, additional curriculum planning sessions may be met with criticism and a lack of enthusiasm. In addition, when working with the public, educators must allow tempo to be a prime element for consideration. Community pulse and readiness to accept change may lag behind the faculty's willingness to act. At the same time, a community may wish to invest effort in new curriculum design while the local faculty is satisfied with the status quo. Thus, analysis of effort capability, coordinated with the willingness of school personnel and the community to allocate time and effort to curriculum design, is another set of factors important in innovation.

Analysis for Change

Those who have curriculum decision-making power at the local level often appear reluctant to institute varied programming because of a basic fear of limited success and its subsequent reflection upon professional images. Even neutrality expresses an individual's response to the planning process. Conversely, some educators labor tenaciously to initiate the latest innovation, often without purpose. Change for the sake of change impedes progress and is to be avoided. Advocates of constant change tend to be extremists. This is one of the possible problems of having private contractors implement programs on a money-back guarantee. The system of the corporation must be implemented at any cost. If this system involves reading or math systems, these subjects will be hammered at regardless of other developmental considerations. Instead, the support should be given to the local professional educators.

There are also some educators who insist that offerings at the elementary school level were adequate in the past and that an extension of the fundamental 3 R's is only added expense of little or no benefit to children. All of these attitudes reflect adult identification and value judgments that are less than adequate even for young children. Professional planners have a tendency to promote and initiate change through manipulation of things and people rather than construction of experiences based upon desired behavioral outcomes. When change is accepted as the only known constant (as it should be), educators' concern lies with providing the learner with competencies which will enable him to become a knowledgeable contributing citizen at each stage of his academic and social development.

Traditionally, instruction has relied upon assimilated content and structured evaluation devices. In formal classroom settings, learners have been passive recipients of data with only infrequent opportunities to participate in dialogue—let alone to be allowed the opportunity to assist in the development of alternative tasks in which the individual could participate and derive success. Usually this diminished pupil participation has been a function of class load; however, this rationale may be a cover for inefficient classroom management.

In order to educate for change, children must have the chance to become secure within insecurity. This mental discipline can be arrived at by assisting each child to develop techniques of analysis of substantive content which are consistently transferable to living-learning situations.

Classroom systems of analysis through problem solving provide repeated opportunities for each child to apply assimilated data while increasing his facility to define, research, classify, hypothesize, experiment, keep records, construct models, summarize, derive valid conclusions, and make recommendations. When a child becomes increasingly proficient in these skills, he soon realizes that many responses can be acceptable. The acceptability of the response depends upon the given or obtainable data and the quality of the ordered systematic analysis. Hence, every child in the elementary school can be successful.

Although assimilated knowledge and level of insight varies among children according to native ability and personal motivation, the mastery of logical analysis applied to relevant problem-solving tasks allows an elementary school child to become an active participant in learning. Continual success based upon flexible and acceptable responses in required and supplementary learning tasks creates a basis for an individual child to become secure. The end product, it is hoped, is an independent learner. Thus, education for change requires a continual analysis by both the teacher and learner so that children armed with self-confidence and skills with which to solve academic and social problems may perceive the unknown as a challenge.

Curriculum for Educational Competency

Along with any curriculum innovation comes the question of evaluation of competency level. Assuming that some type of evaluation is standard procedure, the educator should consider characteristics of the independent learner which relate to humanistic values to be of primary importance to the educational product. That is, the educator seeks to determine the degree to which an independent learner exhibits self-confidence when dealing with unknowns.

Since time is a limiting factor, the courses included in the curriculum should be given severe scrutiny. Delineation of the essential from the non-essential is a daily task for the elementary school teacher. The child's time should be utilized in the acquisition of pertinent information rather than in the accumulation of miscellaneous misinformation. A mastery of information minimals allows for intensive application of competencies; an indescriminate barrage of material may clutter, disrupt order, and even confuse the learner.

Relying on assimilated minimal information provides time for supplementary learning situations in the form of remediation and/or enrichment. There should be opportunities for in-depth interest study and enrichment for all children, providing avenues for creative development. Viewed as a continual self-organizing process, personalized creative learning then is necessary for each child—regardless of ability. All too often bright and gifted youngsters reap rewards of having the choice to enhance their personal worth, while the less able become immersed in the drudgery of fundamentals and seldom experience the excitement and wonder of involvement within the school day. Therefore, "to survey—unclutter—instruct better" can serve as a motto for increasing instructional competency and in turn raising the level of learning by the individual child.

The competency of the independent learner involves many, many factors, but attitudes appear to be the determining element with reference to success. The individual's feelings about himself in a given situation are the catalytic agents which limit or expand the potential outcomes of any given situation. In effect, the attitudes of an individual are responsible for his limited or great success. Ability to assimilate information and apply acquired knowledge depends to a large extent upon an individual's attitudinal set. In the final analysis, formulation of attitudes is a primary function of the elementary school; and the quality and level of academic and social competency is a function of attitude.

Fad-Fashion-Learning

When philosophy, educational objectives, analysis of effort capability, need for change, and bases of competency levels have been agreed upon by all concerned in the instructional process, actual selection of curriculum programming has to take place. Caution must be exercised in order that projects are consistent with established educational goals. Selection ought to be based upon the innovation's potential to increase the quantity and quality of learning for individual children. The popularity of a method, technique, and materials may run a short course and result in undue expenditure of finances and professional effort. Thus, program innovation should be selected for its contribution to change on a long-range basis.

COMPONENTS OF FUNCTIONAL OPERATION

Priority Projects

Because program selection must be essentially long range in orientation, a priority of selection should be determined as a part of initial planning. Rank order is a necessity in so far as logical sequence can affect the structure that carries out educational objectives. In any given school system, all individuals, groups, and departmental specialists tend to believe that all of their suggestions should take precedence; yet this attitude obviously is not practical. Addressing the problem of priority selection at the elementary school level from a systems point of view, priority selection should reflect the most pressing need of a given group of pupils and/or the entire school constituency.

Criteria for establishing rank order should be consistent with individual-oriented educational objectives. Instituting programming should not become a mechanical function. Some questions which will assist educators in arriving at the priority given to any specific innovation are: (1) What educational impact will it have in raising the quality and quantity of learning for the children? (2) How many children will be involved? (3) What resources are required both at the initiation stage and for maintenance in the future? (4) Are there special requirements needed, such as extralegal support, and will the general community support continuation of the programming? (5) Is the faculty professionally ready to assume the new dimensions of this curriculum innovation? (6) Will pupils, parents, and the general community be given ample time for a thorough orientation with reference to rationale for selection, implementation, contribution that it is anticipated to bring about in terms of the school district's educational objectives? Acceptable programming and innovation priority must be determined in order to effectively manage long-range curriculum development.

Phase-In for Continuity

When making programming operational at the local level, many administrators become overly ambitious. Tempo is a crucial element in reasonable management. A phase-in of curriculum change allows any school, regardless of effort capability, to participate fully in curriculum change ranging from the experimental to the adaptive on a small or large scale. In phasing-in a curriculum, readiness is a prime consideration. When priorities have been established, phase-in allows for the firm establishment and maintenance of quality education.

Diversity Within Continuity When teachers and school officials implement new approaches to curriculum at the elementary school level, there is often a concerted effort to *standardize—formalize* the new on a mass scale within a given school system. Method, technique, and materials are instituted in similar form. This limits success; each teacher *should* take the program, available materials, suggested method, and demonstrated technique, and analyze his particular professional responsibility with reference to transfer into learning experiences for one child, small group, or whole class of children. Rigid adherence to demonstrated procedure per se insures limited success. Every teacher must internalize the innovative curriculum and create living-learning situations which are specifically designed for those to whom he is responsible professionally.

Because teachers differ both in professional preparation and facility to operate and use many media in the instructional setting, it is imperative that each person charged with an instructional assignment prepare systematically in terms of agreed content. The principle of phase-in now must be applied at the individual instructional level. Likewise, the total faculty should be made to realize and accept that adaptation of both the content and the method of innovative curriculum will have to be modified with reference to teacher style. This expected variation is a natural evolution and provides for creative application of content, method, and technique. Discouragement of diversity structures the curriculum and serves to thwart the individualization of instruction. Diversity, within continuity, allows the teacher and individual child to identify personally with curriculum change. The amount of quality involvement is thus proportionately enhanced.

Community Orientation and Participation

Community orientation and participation in curriculum development has been mentioned before. In the past, professional educators have excluded the community from planning and participation in curriculum development. Although the professional is vested with the responsibility of making the decisions concerning curriculum innovation, administration and faculty have a reciprocal responsibility to provide opportunities for the community to find out about new programs—their purposes and anticipated outcomes. This can be efficiently undertaken by means of brochures, school newspaper, and small and large group meetings. Most effective are parent-teacher conferences and small discussion groups. Thorough understanding seldom is the result of mass meetings. The members of the community should have an in-depth understanding of curricular issues. Parents are usually made aware of changes by their children, but they appreciate knowing what supportive contribution they can make. Their roles as auxiliary assistants should do much toward extending community understanding of new programming. Another problem is that too frequently those who support the school financially yet have no children in attendance are staunch critics of programs because they hear only half-truths or misinformation. This overlooked element in every community can be a part of those extralegal forces which continually plague both traditional and innovative programs.

Continual orientation programs and requests for purposeful participation of the community can bring continuous dividends, as supportive effort in all forms will be based upon comprehensive knowledge.

Realistic Effort: Now and in the Future

Effort, one factor of program analysis, must be realistically determined in terms of current and future resources. Extravagance cannot be tolerated at any time; calculations that are conservative assist in building credibility between the school personnel and the general community. What is even more important, available effort must be maximized. Favorable and continued community support rests upon demonstrating the professional faculty's concern for and ability to increase quality education for each child with existing means before requesting modification or additional support.

Effort "now" is relatively predictable. The future may be speculative, though based upon reliable data. Caution should be exercised when calculating effort in relation to long-range curriculum development. Innovative programming has repeatedly been only temporary because long-range effort and extralegal forces combined to diminish and eventually terminate worthy projects. Visionary educational leadership coupled with continuous realistic appraisal of effort, present and future, can create a basis for continuity and long-term operation. When innovation has been meticulously internalized and effort correctly assessed, a program can move forward under its own momentum rather than deteriorate into fragments once its prime energizer has left the scene. Insightful analysis requires continual examination and modification for effective on-going innovative programming.

PERSONALIZED CURRICULUM APPLIED

Individualized Instruction a Possibility

Individualized instruction has always been a goal of all who are involved in the instruction of children. However, this goal is easier verbalized than applied; lack of management expertise has caused curriculum to be less than individualized. Preoccupation with things instead of ideas and behavioral outcomes has caused learning experiences to be largely creations of teachers.

Individualized instruction can become functional only when behavioral outcomes are of primary concern. Implicit here is the necessity for the child to be involved in the planning-learning process. Passive involvement, where a child is manipulated throughout the school day, is incompatible with individualized instruction.

Individualization refers to "one, alone, by oneself." By inference, the learner should posses independent study skills, self-motivation, and behavioral control in order to be self-actualizing. Individualized instruction should be viewed not as an education singularity per se, but as the creation of experiences whereby the assessment of a child's educational, social, physical, and spiritual requirements are considered and continually re-examined. In a system of individualized instruction, a given child is educated as an independent learner in several dynamic structures simultaneously: alone; as one among a small group of peers (three to five); as one within a large learning situation such as multigroup or whole class; as one among a group of mixed ages. However, forced independence should not be equated with individualizing learning experiences. Analysis of need in conjunction with perceiving the learner as an individual is the essence of individualized personal curriculum in the elementary school.

Role of the Elementary School Teacher

We have seen that elementary school instruction is still largely teacher-centered and textbook-dominated. The teacher who works to individualize curriculum must assume a new role in the learning process. This present-day teacher at the elementary school level no longer works alone. He is one of an instructional team which includes experts in a substantive content area, reading, and competency in diagnosis of educational need on an individual basis. (See Figure 2.) Each member of the instructional team serves as a consultant in his area of specialization, eliminates the propensity for departmentalization. Although each adult is responsible for a given number of children, instruction relies heavily upon team effort in diagnosis, and is articulated through the instructional media center which now serves as the nerve center for learning.[1] The emerging role of the elementary specialist is one of participation in an instructional team so that the child has the benefit of both the generalist and content specialist. Responsibility for reading instruction and working with other team member specialists makes interrelatedness of subject matter possible because reading skills are common to all subject areas. This approach to curriculum planning more readily insures that a child is learning through his formal study as an active participant instead of assimilating content for no relevant purpose.

---

[1] Although a member of a professional instructional team, the elementary school teacher has a flexible role.

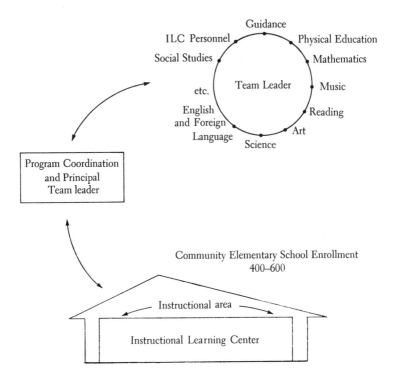

FIGURE 2

Instructional Team of Tomorrow

Conceptual Competency Frame

When considering individualization of instruction, desired conceptual competencies must be delineated. Each teacher has the task of selecting skills and knowledge worthy of knowing and then of preparing appropriate instructional objectives.[2] A single objective must specifically communicate to any learner what he is asked to undertake, state the conditions of the experiences, list how success can be recognized, and include evaluative criteria in order for the learner to know how well he has accomplished the objective. Unfortunately, getting teachers to be precise in writing is difficult. There seems to be a tendency to include

---

[2] Mager's *Preparing Instructional Objectives* is a helpful set of guidelines with which to develop specific objectives.

content and assignments in formal study, but the selection of essential skills and knowledge which will provide for an orderly system for study, utilizing multi-media as tools for personalized learning, poses problems for most teachers.

Mastery of Minimals

Surveying the standard curriculum presented at the elementary school level, there is an enormous amount of material included. Because of the need for skill and concept proficiency combined with a tendency to shorten the school day, selection of specific objectives is increasingly important. Organized learning experiences allow for increased flexibility of pupil involvement by design. Contrary to popular notion, flexibility is a natural outcome of structure. Establishing performance objectives delimits learning experiences to that degree that minimals, in a conceptual framework, can be commanded to mastery. In the past, concepts have been submerged in quantity coverage; but selected minimal concepts, thoroughly comprehended, can always be applied to quantity. The urgency to "finish the book" which permeates many classrooms may at the same time be a primary reason for academic confusion.

Working with minimal performance objectives releases time for adjunctive exploration. This available time can be extended by creation of a broader dimension to instructional analysis. Currently, performance objectives, though specific, tend to fragment learning where the learner does not comprehend interrelationships of skills and concepts throughout his courses of study.[3]

A teacher must literally "rethink instructional order." This task may be a relatively long-term process because most teachers have not experienced learning in an interrelated format at any stage of their formal study—inclusive of professional preparation. When living–learning experiences are a series of comprehended interrelationships, the purpose of learning as an agent of self-improvement can become increasingly meaningful beginning at the elementary level of instruction.

The Sequence of Study

During the elementary school years, a child works with increasingly more difficult tools for the purpose of acquiring and assimilating knowledge. Learning should be undertaken in sequence. Criterion performance objectives present a means to assist every teacher and learner to create a personal sequence within the total living-learning environment. A

---

[3] See Appendix. A, pp. 105-6.

systematic progression understood by both the teacher and learner creates a basis for more comprehensive interaction between and among teachers and learners. Sequence firms up order; the teacher's instructional security transfers to a child-learner. The transfer results in the teacher's increased willingness to allow the learner to participate more actively in his own course of study with reference both to content and to his role as an active independent learner.

Independent Study Skills and Learning Independence

Individualized instruction and its ultimate success are dependent on each child's knowledge of and competency to utilize study skills in the acquisition of knowledge and subsequent problem solving. Those factors which create independence are a composite of skills that modify an individual's behavior and are not mastered in one academic year. Astute analysis is necessary on the part of the educator-specialist so that each child will be able to participate in those activities which he can undertake successfully. Again, a phase-in is fundamental in developing learning independence. A continual opportunity to participate in supervised interrelated learning activities which require several media is the single vehicle whereby an individual child can acquire those independent study skills that allow him the best possible opportunity of becoming a self-actualizing learner.

Instructional Media

Although an instructional media center and special personnel are desirable, the availability of instructional media is the crucial issue. Just because physical plant does not provide space for centralized accessability, the utilization of media should not be excluded from a curriculum. Since children learn in different ways, each child should be encouraged and assisted to develop his own style of learning. This attitude demands that diverse approaches which utilize several media should be common at the elementary school level. Unfortunately, use of audio-visual materials often begins and ends with teacher-instruction. In order to follow through and support independent learning, each child should be required to use different media as learning tools in both supervised and independent study.

While teachers and administrators may be hesitant to allow elementary school children to use hardware for independent study, when provided with supervised instruction, elementary school children can efficiently operate audio-visual equipment.[4] There seems to exist a notion that an

---

[4] An elementary school child can learn to operate and use correctly the following

elementary school child will break or incorrectly use equipment. Observation of elementary school children proves otherwise. In fact, one might suggest that, when taught correctly, they possess a high level of operational facility. Thus, if inclusion of audio-visual materials is recommended in teacher-instruction, it follows that these same instructional materials can be used as independent learning tools in individualized instruction.

Emphasis has been placed on hardware utilization because these materials are necessary if individualized instruction is to be the pace-setting educational goal during this decade. Software has been utilized with children as a learning tool; however, adherence to texts and encyclopedias limits even the use of software. Often these materials are housed in particular classrooms, and other staff members are unaware of their existence. In effect, there are thousands of items held by classroom teachers that are inaccessible beyond the local building level. If space does not permit centralization, the faculty should be provided with an index of titles, location, and procedures for procurement so that the child can select from a more comprehensive offering. In this way teachers also have expanded resources with which to plan and carry out the objectives of the curriculum.

Final Evaluation

Hopefully, grades per se can be eventually eliminated. Undue emphasis on grades causes a learner to strive for the evaluation outcome rather than for knowledge for self-improvement. Students should acquire knowledge for its usefulness instead of just learning to pass a test and then promptly forgetting all the new material. In an individualized curriculum, each child will undertake a given task until he has demonstrated to his teacher the required level of competency.[5] In the traditional system, acceptable, at the minimal level, would be the grade of (C). As

---

hardware: film and filmstrip projectors, tape recorders, single concept loop viewers, slide projectors, stereo record players, language masters, controlled readers, and overhead and opaque projectors.

[5] When ability, rate of assimilation, and factors of self-motivation are considered, a child can succeed. He will be encouraged to work in those areas which build skill competencies from which his success is observable to himself. Increased self-value is a potent factor in motivation. Each teacher must keep in mind that many of his pupils will never go to college, but many may require additional study to become successful in business and trades. Our purpose is to provide relevant study so that there are no potential drop-outs. A child "fails" when curricula, teacher attitudes, and external factors combine to block his success. When an independent learner awaits teacher guidance, not a system of obstacles which create despair, in time deep-seated academic and social problems which can affect an individual's life accomplishment can be eliminated.

an individual learner, a child may elect the level of competency he wishes to achieve. This situation in itself takes much of the stress out of the learning process and frees a child to pursue his learning tasks, knowing that he will succeed. Regardless of ability, some children need more time than others to assimilate knowledge. In an individualized curriculum, there is time for each child to compete with himself in a relaxed atmosphere.

To achieve higher levels of excellence, any student may pursue supplementary study which allows him to branch out from the mainstream of minimal concepts to investigate related subjects. (See Appendix C, pp. 109-10) Again, once the learner has fulfilled a performance criterion, the final evaluation agreed upon is automatic. Thus, accurate diagnosis of need, ability, rate of assimilation, and factors affecting self-motivation must form a nucleus for day-to-day analysis. The highly specific diagnosis, by a single teacher or skilled teaching team, provides data with which to properly place pupils in skills areas, and to assure sequence in learning tasks.[6]

Contracts

At this time, contract method–individual project (IP's) may be thought to be synonomous with individualized instruction. However, the contract–individual project is simply a statement in writing which serves to clarify any given work assignment. It serves as a document for reference when misunderstanding occurs. There is a tendency for contracts to be a narrow-based format that fragments the curriculum. Built on skill competencies, few contracts are designed as cumulative experiences which allow a learner to use interrelated knowledge. There is a need to include not only a skills function but those experiences in which a child can apply his assimilated knowledge.

Examination of contracts-individual projects prepared for elementary school children illustrate the fact that the language is "teacher language" which could confuse rather than clarify. The format is forced and mechanical. Precision of word choice should be exercised when writing for children. Critical thinking must precede writing performance criteria, evaluative criteria, and instructional resources. Purpose and classification should be implicit within the statement of a performance criterion. Instructional resources may appear to be merely a list rather than a carefully designated grouping to encourage utilization of several media.

---

[6] Although sequence provides internal order to study, a child should be provided with an opportunity to demonstrate his knowledge. When acceptable proficiency has been demonstrated, he should be exempt from sequence and allowed to advance accordingly.

Specific and *complete* entries should be consistently noted. If a teacher-led presentation (TLP) is included, list the topic or specifics to be covered rather than just TLP. Avoid using such phrases as "See IP 2," and "Same as before." Rewrite citations each time. Simple coding such as (*) before an entry signifies required use; the remainder then is optional. All too often, the contract–individual project is the old course of study—text and workbook—in contract format. (See Appendix B, pp. 107-8.)

Individualized instruction within the contract format is of course desirable but the amount of effort required to prepare materials is a formidable task for many teachers. Therefore, alternate vehicles must be developed if individualized instruction is to become operational in elementary school curriculum. Because time is an omnipresent factor in preparation, teachers should concentrate on four major tasks:

(1) Developing a clear statement of performance objectives which include what is to be undertaken with given resources, and how; and to what level the learner's work will be evaluated.

(2) Including sample criteria which cue the learner as to the type and level of accuracy that will be acceptable. Percentiles do not always apply. Presented assignments can best be evaluated in a conference where the child has the opportunity to explain and demonstrate his assimilated knowledge on a pass–no pass basis. Many IP's include subheadings of *Sample Test Situation*. This subheading may present evaluation vehicles in the form of traditional paper and pencil examinations. In order to increase independent learning, alternative ways of evaluation, even within a single lesson, should be permissible. Teachers must remember that quantity—finger exercises–time fillers—has nothing to do with quality performance. Accent excellence on minimals to keep the momentum of self-motivation maximized. (See Appendix C, pp. 110-11.)

(3) Including application and invention in the plan. In the main, learning experiences have leveled off at knowledge and comprehension and occasionally application. Moreover, directed study as currently practiced in most elementary schools limits opportunities for application; seldom is invention encouraged. Because of the flexible nature of individualizing curriculum, contracts—individual projects should be written consistently at the level of application and invention. At the invention level, an independent learner can exercise his creative organizing abilities which are fundamental to self-fulfillment.[7]

---

[7] When creativity is viewed as essentially an act of personal organization, everyone becomes an active participant at individual levels of insight based upon skill competency and assimilated knowledge.

(4) Giving primary consideration to resources in consonance with performance criteria. Care should be exercised to include appropriate materials and not to list materials indiscriminately, which destroys the orderliness of the contract–individual project. All listed resources should be available to the learner. In situations where resources are limited, such as small rural schools, the children may possess resources that they would be willing to share.

Modification and adaptation of contract–individual projects can be encouraged, depending upon local circumstances. Although most teachers use a published format, an indexed tape would possibly serve as efficiently and conserve teacher planning time. In the final analysis, *format per se is not the primary concern.* Teacher thought process, specifically expressed in written or oral performance criteria, is fundamental when individualizing the curriculum at the elementary school level.

Records and Pupil Change

Due to the flexible nature of individualized instruction, conventional recording procedures are no longer appropriate means of evaluating pupil change.[8] Because learning has been individualized, ways in which each pupil is evaluated must be personalized too. Skills can be placed on duplicated forms, dated, and initialed when acceptable competency has been demonstrated. Anecdotal records can describe observable behavior in several situations; over a period of time, patterns of behavior begin to appear. Each child can assist the teacher in keeping informal records of such achievements as programmed reading and books read. A folder containing representative work of each child provides a primary source with which to describe strengths and limitations, both academic and social. These folders should be periodically weeded out so that they retain order.

Letters can be helpful in interpreting pupil change to parents. Faculty and administration may agree that by a certain date each parent will have received a minimum of one evaluation letter. Informing parents of academic and social strengths and limitations as each becomes apparent will be appreciated. When letters are sent to parents, the following sequence may serve as a guide for content organization:

(1) Describe specific instances which illustrate acceptable or better competencies, both academic and social.

---

[8] "Pupil change" has been used rather than "pupil progress" because a child may not always progress. He may remain relatively unchanged—academically and/or socially—or there may be a loss recorded in skills knowledge as measured by standardized tests.

(2) Delineate one or two areas which need improvement and suggest ways in which parents can be of assistance and what the school personnel is doing to assist the child.

(3) Include a summary statement.

(4) Invite parents to the school for a conference.

A letter which follows this outline, supported by specific illustrations and worded in precise terms, can cause parents to support the school because their child's evaluation is oriented to him as an individual.[9] (See Appendix D, pp. 112-17.)

The teacher who can convey genuine interest accurately and convey pupil change with empathy can be a vital force in the education of every child. This ability to communicate with a child also can help the child and his parents to communicate. As a result, the child has understanding support from both his teacher and parents, support which allows him to continue on in his quest to become an independent learner. Regardless of the quality and level of the testing tools, they indicate change at a given time. No evaluation is permanent; performance over time affords greater accuracy of predictability. Human variables cause all evaluations to be less than perfect.

Teacher Supervision

Assuming that a teacher has developed a curriculum thoughtfully, the success of individualized instruction as an operational organization for learning is dependent upon the teacher's expertise in supervision. Independence is a desired attribute of each learner; however, this same independent learner needs consistent guidance in his study. Regardless of ability, supervision must be astutely exercised in making sure that each child has completed his work within the agreed upon limits. All of the previous planning is of little consequence if assigned projects, either individual or team-oriented, are allowed to be prepared haphazardly. Knowing that his teacher consistently expects his best, a child will try when provided with thorough instruction and encouragement.

As a continual activity, supervision of follow-up is the one factor of learning that seems to be severely neglected. After successfully complet-

---

[9] Letters to parents must be thoughtfully prepared. When several are written at one time, they tend to become general, less personalized, and of little specific value. Those school administrators who provide confidential stenographic assistants for the faculty will find their faculties more willing to write evaluation letters to parents. In order to insure continuity, such a program allows the principal to read the letters before issuance. By doing so, he becomes informed of data relative to individual children. This practice places him in a position to provide professional support and guidance when called upon by a teacher.

ing an individual or team project, the students should ask such questions as, "Where do we go from here?" and "What affect do the findings have on. . . ?" By including follow-up activities as logical extensions of basic study, the act of independent learning goes full cycle.

Supervision of a child or groups of children within individualized instruction is manifested in an informal manner by the teacher. Critical observation is a primary component of effective instruction. The ability to observe work habits, recognize anxiety levels, and analyze applied skill competency and knowledge without being obvious are qualities of supervision which each teacher should cultivate. Likewise, listening is essential. Accurate interpretation of what is said in contrast to the original meaning raises the communication level and provides a more valid basis upon which judgments can be formulated. Often an informal conference or discussion with a child-study team is an appropriate setting for counsel. An independent learner desires guidance and supervision rather than arbitrary work assignments and teacher abdication.

Evaluation of Individualized Instruction

A curriculum designed for individualized independent learning places a high priority upon mastered minimals and supplementary study. Curriculum planning takes into consideration an individual child's ability and rate of assimilation and allows for multimedia activities within an assigned area of study. Because this curriculum design attempts to provide for the many variables of human learning, the conventional standardized tests may not measure the knowledge assimilated or the human values derived from individualized instruction. Thus, standardized tests may not include the skills or subject matter that pupils within this type of curriculum have studied.

Emphasis on ability and rate shatters the grade-level concept. This learning environment places priority on skill competency and creation of attitudes toward self and learning. Therefore, if tests must be administered, those that reveal attitudes should be most useful in trying to evaluate success of the program. When a school district changes to a curriculum oriented to the individual, skill scores may dip below national norms because of the necessity of adjustment of both teachers and children to a new concept of instruction and learning. Conversely, when supervision and classroom management exhibit organized flexibility, an individual should be able to become a more able student than when he was a directed learner in a teacher-centered, textbook-centered, graded classroom.

Curriculum should be designed for specific communities of children. When a curriculum is designed for a specific child or group of children, local curriculum planners are obligated to create their own evaluative tools. Since individualized instruction depends to a large extent upon utilization of many media, a challenge confronts every teacher to develop and allow a child to demonstrate academic competency in a multimedia format. Hence, in order to evaluate learning, teachers have a professional responsibility to provide a child with evaluation instruments that honestly attempt to measure the individual child's accomplishment. (See Appendix D, pp. 112-17.)

SUMMARY

Curriculum development should be a response to continual change. Based upon educational philosophy and objectives, effort capability, and analysis for change, learning experiences that are desirable for the children of a given community can be realistically planned. Establishing a priority on innovation selection and applying a phase-in policy are essential activities that insure diversity and continuity. Involving and continually informing the taxpaying public coupled with realistically appraising both current and future efforts are major continuous activities for education planners, if they wish innovation in curriculum to be long-lasting.

Individualized instruction as an on-going learning format allows each child an opportunity to study, free from stresses which accompany the more formalized graded grouping of children. The level and quality of success hinges upon establishing performance criteria in terms of minimal understanding in consonance with consistent diagnosis by a cooperative instructional team. In addition, expertise in informal supervision, educational management, and selection of appropriate means of evaluation are prerequisites to the success of a fundamental curriculum designed with concern for the ability and rate of knowledge assimilation of each child.

Major Themes

1. Curriculum development and its effective implementation should be constructed in consonance with educational philosophy and objectives of the local school district.

2. An analysis of effort capability is essential if curriculum planning is to be realistic.

3. Change, being a constant, causes educational planners to carefully analyze existing offerings in order that selected innovation is relevant, and complements and maximizes existing expended effort by raising both the quality and quantity of instruction.

4. Curriculum offerings at any local school should allow each child an opportunity to acquire the level of competency desired in terms of the instructional faculty's educational objectives.

5. Curriculum development should consistently be based upon educational need rather than fad and fashion.

6. Priority project selection and phase-in policy provide a basis for diversified continuity.

7. Continual community orientation and participation in curriculum planning assists in creating an informed and supporting public.

8. Community effort, now and in the future, should be continually evaluated if curriculum innovation and modification is to be sustained for a long period of time.

9. Like all other organizations for learning, individualized instruction is an attitude toward learning where pupil-centered learning experiences are a mode of evaluation.

10. The elementary school teacher's new role is one of participation in an instructional team as a broad area specialist with expertise in reading instruction.

11. For efficient continuity, performance criteria involving delineated minimals and use of many media are a fundamental responsibility for each member of the instructional team at the elementary school level.

12. Sequence of study and independent study skills are fundamental to individualized instruction and learning independence.

13. An instructional media center, decentralized or centralized, serving as a repository of hardware/software and study areas is the nerve center for pupil learning and teacher planning. Accessibility to appropriate multimedia materials is essential to initiate and maintain individualized instruction.

14. Concern for learning ability and rate of assimilating knowledge should provide an individual learner with an opportunity to participate in broadening supplementary study.

15. Continual diagnosis of educational competency provides data with which to assist each child to achieve academic excellence at his current ability and achievement level.

16. Individual contracts (IP = individual project) tend to fragment curriculum and often lack flexible choice of media with which to perform the performance criterion.

17. Traditional reporting practices tend not to be appropriate for individualized instruction. Conferences and letters provide more acceptable means for flexible and specific description and illustration of pupil change.

18. Consistent supervision is fundamental to quality educational management where a learner desires guidance in contrast to forced premature learning independence.

19. Conventional and standardized testing vehicles may not effectively evaluate a child's assimilated knowledge because of the attempt to provide learning experiences for a wide range of learning variables.

20. Each member of the instructional team is obligated to create evaluative tools to measure academic and social competencies of a child at the local school level.

SUPPLEMENTARY READINGS

Alexander, W. M., et. al., *The Emergent Middle School* (New York: Holt, Rinehart and Winston, 1970).

Allender, J. S., "Some Determinants of Inquiry Activity in Elementary School Children," *Journal of Educational Psychology*, Vol. 61 (June, 1970), pp. 220–25.

Berman, Louise M., *New Priorities in Curriculum* (Columbus, Ohio: Charles E. Merrill Publishing Company, 1968).

Brakken, E., "Inquiry Involves Individualizing," *Instructor*, Vol. 78 (October, 1968), pp. 78, 95 ff.

Burns, R. W., and G. D. Brooks, "Designing Curriculum in a Changing Society," *Educational Technology*, Vol. 10 (April, 1970), pp. 7–57.

Crosby, M., "Who Changes the Curriculum and How?" *Phi Delta Kappan*, Vol. 51 (March, 1970), pp. 385–89.

Estvan, F. J., "Teaching the Very Young, Procedures for Developing Inquiring Skills," *Phi Delta Kappan*, Vol. 50 (March, 1969), pp. 383–93.

Goodlad, John, "Curriculum: A Janus Look," *The Record*, Vol. 70, No. 2 (November, 1968), pp. 95–107.

Jerman, M., "Computers, Instruction and the Curriculum," *Educational Technology*, Vol. 10 (May, 1970), pp. 53–56.

Joyce, Bruce R., *Alternative Models of Elementary Education* (Waltham, Mass.: Ginn/Blaisdell, 1969).

Kapfer, P. G., "Behavioral Objectives and the Curriculum Processor," *Educational Technology*, Vol. 10 (May, 1970), pp. 14–17.

Krathwohl, David R., "Stating Objectives Appropriately for Program, for Curriculum and for Instructional Materials Development," *Journal of Teacher Education*, Vol. 16 (1965), pp. 83–92.

Mager, Robert F., *Developing Attitude Toward Learning* (Palo Alto, Calif.: Fearon Publishers, 1968).

————, *Preparing Instructional Objectives* (Palo Alto, Calif.: Fearon Publishers, 1962).

Metcalf, L. E. and M. P. Hunt, "Relevance and the Curriculum," *Phi Delta Kappan*, Vol. 51 (March, 1970), pp. 358–61.

Raths, L., S. Wasserman, A. Jonas, and A. M. Rothstein, *Teaching for Thinking: Theory and Application* (Columbus, Ohio: Charles E. Merrill Publishing Company, 1967).

Suppes, P., "Computers in the Classroom: Handling Student Differences," *Education Digest*, Vol. 33 (October, 1967), pp. 8–10.

Torrance, E. P., "Uniqueness and Creativeness: The School's Role," *Educational Leadership* (1967), pp. 493–96.

Tyre, K. A., "Principal as a Change Agent," *National Elementary Principal*, Vol. 49 (February, 1970), pp. 41–51.

Tyler, Ralph W., "New Dimensions in Curriculum Development," *Phi Delta Kappan* (September, 1966), pp. 25–28.

Wolfson, B. J. and S. Nash, "Perceptions of Decision-Making in Elementary School Classrooms," *Elementary School Journal*, Vol. 69 (November, 1968), pp. 89–93.

5

NON - TEACHING ROLES OF THE TEACHER

THE GUIDANCE FUNCTION

Nature of Elementary School Guidance[1]

Complementing the instructional aspect of the elementary school is the emerging concept of elementary school guidance. Where secondary school guidance programs are chiefly concerned with vocational guidance, in the elementary school guidance is focused upon an individual child within the total matrix of classroom activity.[2] While a child is developing personal independence as a learner, he remains dependent upon adults for direction throughout the elementary school years. Thus, cooperative working relationships between teacher and parents play a strategic role in a child's adjustment to and ultimate success at school.

Guidance at the elementary school level is oriented toward diagnosis, with continual identification of problems. (See Figure 3.) This should be kept in mind at the time of curriculum design. As Kopp and McNeff point out, in the past and even now, much effort has been expended by administration, professional faculty, and parents in gathering diagnostic data; but its analysis and the subsequent conclusions seldom get translated into minimal programs which honestly assist the individual child.

In order to assist the individual child, the circle of problem identification must be broken and the known data must be utilized in seeking a solution to the child's problem. The two-step plan set forth by Kopp

---

[1] This section is based on Kopp and McNeff, *Guidance Handbook, op. cit.,* pp. 15–19.

[2] *Ibid.,* pp. 15–16. "Whenever it is practical, the guidance counselor works with teachers in providing guidance services to children."

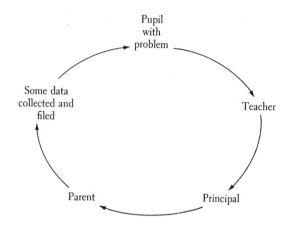

FIGURE 3

Endless Circle of Problem Identification

Source: O. W. Kopp and M. E. McNeff, *Guidance Handbook for Personnel of Elementary Schools* (Lincoln, Nebr.: University of Nebraska Press, 1969).

and McNeff provides a practical suggestion for action: (1) diagnosis and (2) a plan for action based upon diagnosis.[3] Guidance in the elementary school has as its primary concern the early diagnosis of a child's problem, adequate therapy, and the return of the child to his classroom for normal participation with his peers. (See Figure 4.)

Role of the Classroom Teacher in Problem Identification

The key factor to all guidance within the classroom is the child's teacher, because the teacher creates an environment where his attitudes toward a child and learning are ever-present. The counselor and teacher work cooperatively toward creating reasonable learning experiences for those children in need of assistance. Independent action on the part of a teacher is discouraged, but *synergistic action* (described by Kopp and McNeff) accents the desirable cooperation required for maximum results.[4] (See Figure 5, p. 70.)

Classroom teachers basically have the duty of referral, either formal or informal. Usually children have a combination of personal problems

---

[3] *Ibid.,* p. 19.
[4] *Ibid.,* p. 24.

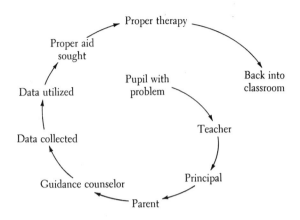

FIGURE 4

Breaking Out of Endless Circle

Source: O. W. Kopp and M. E. McNeff, *Guidance Handbook for Personnel of Elementary Schools* (Lincoln, Nebr.: University of Nebraska Press, 1969).

which combine to impair their judgment and progress at school.[5] When problems are not easily identified, an empathetic teacher should elicit the assistance of an elementary school counselor.

GUIDANCE FUNCTION AND INDIVIDUALIZATION OF INSTRUCTION

As a member of an instructional team, a teacher has the opportunity to observe the whole child in his daily activities at school. (See Figure 2.) From this vantage point, he can collect data that allows him to interpret the behavior of a child. Thus, each teacher has information to be shared in order that an accurate diagnosis and program of assistance and/or therapy can be prescribed.[6]

In order to create an effective curriculum in which each individual child can be successful, personal problems must be isolated and solved.

---

[5] Kopp and McNeff include 38 personal problems (as interpreted by children) which represent those problems that commonly occur in any elementary school which should be considered when planning of learning experiences for individual children.

[6] *Ibid.*, pp. 36–37.

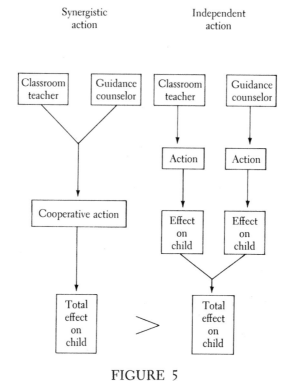

FIGURE 5

Synergistic Versus Independent Action

Source: O. W. Kopp and M. E. McNeff, *Guidance Handbook for Personnel of Elementary Schools* (Lincoln, Nebr.: University of Nebraska Press, 1969).

The identification of personal problems and their subsequent solutions are fundamental to planning for pupil involvement. From kindergarten through the sixth level, each teacher plays a significant role in diagnosing and following through, once a plan of action has been initiated. Instructional efforts are then programmed in an individualized format.[7] (See Appendix E, pp. 118-24.)

---

[7] Dr. Marie O. McNeff, Assistant Professor, Augsburg College, Minneapolis, Minnesota, has prepared three sample studies for inclusion and analysis. Each study represents a possible situation that an elementary classroom teacher could be called upon to seek solutional The case studies are: (1) "Need For Guidance At Elementary Level?—You Be the Judge"; (2) "Martin," which illustrates teacher-counselor cooperation; (3) "Susan," which illustrates the cooperative efforts of the entire instructional team, specialists, and community agency personnel.

INSTRUCTIONAL MATERIALS CENTER:
NERVE CENTER FOR LEARNING

Curriculum design for personalized learning and individualized instruction is dependent upon an instructional materials center (also called an instructional media center). The operational philosophy of a materials center is built upon (1) *quality* in resources, staff, and facilities; (2) *service* to students and teachers; and (3) *balance* in the distribution of function and media.[8] An instructional materials center in an elementary school is more than a library hinged to an audio-visual center. Such a functional media collection should include all of the printed materials usually housed in a school library and an audio-visual center, all properly catalogued.

Beggs states that "An Instructional Materials Center (IMC) is a place where ideas, in their multimedia and diverse forms, are housed, used, and distributed to classrooms and laboratories throughout the school. The IMC contains books, magazines, pamphlets, films, filmstrips, maps, pictures, electronic tapes, recordings, slides, transparencies, mockups, and learning programs."[9] Accepting Beggs' definition, the IMC is the core repository from which pupil-teacher planning and learning take place. Availability of the housed software and hardware is a prerequisite for decentralized learning—which is basic to organizing an individualized curriculum.

Creative Inquiry

Curiosity, an extension of self-motivation, sustains an individual in his attempts to acquire information and solve relevant problems daily. In order to capitalize on this initiative, students must be educated in those skills which allow them to learn on their own.[10] Therefore, an instructional media center has only one reason for existence: to provide those facilities and services which assist in teaching children the methods of creative inquiry.[11] There the individual should feel free to select and exchange materials daily. In these beginning years of supervised study, each child should come to perceive the IMC as a center for learning and

---

[8] William B. Oglesby, "Basic Elements of Instructional Resource Center," *American School and University*, Vol. 40 (May, 1968), p. 59.

[9] David W. Beggs, "Organization Follows Use . . . The Instructional Materials Center," *Audiovisual Instruction*, Vol. 9 (November, 1964), p. 602.

[10] Kenneth I. Taylor, "Creative Inquiry and the School IMC," *Audiovisual Instruction*, Vol. 14 (September, 1969), p. 52.

[11] Virginia Tozier, "The Child and the Library Center," *Educational Leadership*, Vol. XXI (January, 1964), p. 261.

to consistently enjoy the opportunity to develop the habit of utilizing software/hardware. This habit should serve a child well in more formal years of study.[12] Learning and retention will be enhanced when teachers accept the fact that more than one sense should be involved in acquiring information. The teacher who uses the IMC to aid his students' learning of the methods and processes of creative inquiry has another tool for diversifying and individualizing elementary education.

Learning Centers and Guidance An instructional media center is a natural setting for guidance. The function of such a center is to locate, gather, and coordinate a school's material and equipment for learning.[13] The IMC should be a focal point of an activity. When a teacher no longer lectures, he becomes a director or guide of learning experiences. An IMC serves as an invaluable means through which instructional teams can observe and guide the individual. Through careful diagnosis of problems, the teacher can steer students to the most advantageous use of the IMC.[14]

Creative inquiry, self-control, intellectual honesty, and the capacity to think clearly are desirable outcomes which can be acquired through the IMC. These outcomes are an outgrowth of team analysis and skillful administrative procedure. As Gardner points out, "the quality of the teacher is the key to good education."[15] The IMC's function in guidance is in the learning process which hinges upon the teacher as catalytic agent in the coordinated effort.

Maximum Use of the IMC Even though a school may have an IMC, it may not be used by the faculty. Often instructional materials remain unpacked in storage. To encourage use, all available items should be listed in an appropriate index file, with a card index organized in units of work, so that teachers and pupils can use the instructional media center more efficiently.[16]

A teacher today can no longer view audio-visual aids merely as supplementary equipment, if he is to begin to approach his creative

---

[12] Robert S. Gilchrist and Willard G. Jones, "The Instructional Program and the Library," *Theory Into Practice*, Vol. 6 (February, 1967), pp. 5, 7.

[13] James W. Brown and Kenneth Norberg, *Administering Educational Media* (New York: McGraw-Hill Book Company, 1965), p. 264.

[14] Lillian Spitzer, "Looking at Center for Learning Through Research–Colored Glasses," *Educational Leadership*, Vol. XXI (January, 1964), pp. 251–59.

[15] John Gardner, "National Goals in Education," *Goals for Americans* (New York: Prentice-Hall, Inc., 1960), p. 8. This is the Report of the President's Commission on *National Goals*.

[16] William R. Smith, "Indexing Instructional Materials for Greater Teacher Use," *Audiovisual Instruction*, Vol. XI (March, 1966), p. 218.

potential in classroom instruction. Because audio-visual equipment is available, what used be hum-drum can take on new appeal through library references, filmstrips, films, single concept loops, transparencies, tapes, and other teacher-made software.[17] Each classroom teacher must now accept the fact that the intellectually curious child will never again accept a single-text approach to learning.[18]

An instructional media center can be used only as widely as the imagination of the planner. Shores remind us that . . . "half of knowledge is knowing where to find it . . ." This adage has even more significance today as information continues to stockpile.[19] In order to capitalize on effective pupil-teacher communication, an IMC should be open continually throughout the school day. For some communities, the resource center should remain open during the evening and on Saturday to provide services for the whole learning community.[20]

Support for Learning Independence Significant to learning independence is the degree to which a child has functional knowledge of research skills. As part of an instructional team, IMC personnel can best aid children in utilizing available resources when library instruction is consistently related to curriculum content and assignments which require utilization of multimedia resources. In this way, both group and individual guidance can be provided.[21]

When a resource center, properly indexed, is provided and a child comprehends the mechanics of locating knowledge within the IMC, learning independence is fostered. However, the possession of research skills can diminish initiative when the curriculum does not include a required continual use of many media. Hence, ". . . it is through total involvement with the curriculum and faculty, supplemented by community educational agencies, that IMC provides its greatest service to the instruction."[22]

Quality Education on a Mass Scale

When the single textbook and teacher-lecture approach give way to individualized instruction backed up by an instructional team and an

[17] Charles E. Luminati, "Your Equipment Can Be Better and Easier," *The Instructor*, Vol. LXXV (June/July, 1966), p. 62.

[18] Pennsylvania, Department of Public Instruction, *The School Instructional Materials Center and the Curriculum*, 1962, p. 1.

[19] Louis Shores, *Instructional Materials* (New York: The Ronald Press Company, 1960), p. 340.

[20] Margaret Nicholson, "I.M.C.," *School Libraries*, Vol. 13 (March, 1964), p. 42.

[21] Frances Henne, "Learning to Learn in School Libraries," *School Libraries*, Vol. 15 (May, 1966), p. 22.

[22] *The School Instructional Materials Center and the Curriculum*, op. cit., p. 7.

IMC, the quality and variety of learning experiences should improve on a mass scale. Norberg writes that a "functioning media program requires . . . a whole school which is committed to the kind of systematic planning, coordination," and integration of functions that becomes necessary as education moves away from the traditional, self-contained, one-teacher classroom.[23]

Quality education on a mass scale can be a reality with a basis of a flexible curriculum which should include a guidance approach and an IMC. Regardless of available educational effort at the local level, a school faculty that desires to move from a traditional library to an IMC must involve all persons concerned with curriculum development in the effort, in order to coordinate professional expertise in the creation of learning experiences which accent individualization.[24]

MANAGEMENT OF LEARNING EXPERIENCES

Pupil-Centered Instruction and Reorientation of Teacher Management

Throughout the nation, teachers who consider themselves flexible in attitude are the central figures in learning processes. These well meaning people often inadvertently diminish their effectiveness because they provide so many cues and such excessive assistance that fundamental thinking and grappling with problems are not required of the students. In the name of organized efficiency, a classroom teacher may, in effect, tell too much. Through too much lecture in instruction, the teacher forgets that ". . . the optimum learning situation is probably one in which the student is learning how to learn by his own senses."[25]

Goodman reminds us that education should assist one to "become all he is capable of being," and not have ". . . an equal opportunity of becoming carbon copies of ourselves."[26] Teacher-centered classrooms perpetuate mold casting. When a teacher accepts the fact that each child wants to be himself, his repeated failure is replaced by learning success. Throughout the ages conformity has met with resistance by youth; their behavioral response remains the same today.

[23] Kenneth Norberg, "The Challenge of the New Media Standards," *Audiovisual Instruction,* Vol. 14 (September, 1969), p. 20.

[24] Billy K. Pate, "Beginning an Instructional Materials Center," *Michigan Educational Journal,* Vol. XLI (February, 1964), p. 30.

[25] Wilhemine R. Nielson, "Experiences and Language Development," *Childhood Education,* Vol. 46 (December, 1969), p. 136.

[26] Kenneth S. Goodman, "On Valuing Diversity in Language," *Childhood Education,* Vol. 46 (December, 1969), p. 126.

Pupil-centered classrooms allow children to be involved in initial decision making concerning learning experiences, including what, when, and how an individual, group, or whole class may participate. Being allowed to participate in planning and having an opportunity to exercise alternative decisions which affect their learning participation is fundamental to the students' sense of a positive learning environment. A teacher should allow himself to reorient his thinking and assist a child to think, make choices, and err as legitimate acceptable acts within the learning process. Work noise, a slight buzzing, and movement alert the observer to a lively learning situations. In a pupil-centered school, a classroom is a place to learn how to "talk, listen, write, spell, and read."[27] Here in this learning environment, individual children should develop their self-images by being "mathematical wizards, beginning scientists, potential baseball stars, good citizens, and creative in all the arts."[28] For many teachers the challenge is to reevaluate pupil-teacher relationships during this learning process.

Emergence and Guidance of Independent Learning Experiences

Today's pupil-centered curriculum should emphasize independent learning experiences. Many teachers' classrooms have interest centers and project areas which compliment the resources located in an IMC. With knowledge obtained from the instructional team analysis, guidance continually reinforces the individual child so that successful learning creates increased independence. In contrast to past decades, when teachers usually made most (if not all) decisions concerning learning experiences, teachers are now changing their instructional behavior. A teacher in the elementary school should guide a child to discover ". . . the structure of knowledge, the manner and thought processes involved, and the kinds of problems which, when investigated, will open up to the student concepts and understandings vital to his development."[29]

To a minimal extent, common knowledge may be desirable; however, much of the daily fabric of life that inspires youth toward noble ambition and deeds has been the result of independent learning experiences. With this area of curriculum development receiving more consideration by faculty planners, the quality of teacher-guidance is more crucial to

27 Betty L. Broman, "Too Much Shushing—Let Children Talk," *Childhood Education*, Vol. 46 (December, 1969), p. 132.

28 *Ibid.*

29 Willard J. Congreve, "Learning Center . . . Catalyst for Change?" *Educational Leadership*, Vol. XXI (January, 1964), p. 212.

the coordination of independent learning experiences for individuals and groups of children. Accurate data must be obtained with which to appropriately counsel children. Periodic interest inventories administered to pupils alert the teacher to current interests of the children, so that a child can be channeled into those activities of high interest level. As a result, the child may become a more willing learner and undertake and complete his work at an increased level of competence. (See Appendix F, pp. 125-26.)

Differential Grouping for Personalized Instruction

Personalized instruction as a concept has been articulated in a series of activities where forced independence may have been foisted prematurely upon a child. *Differential grouping* is a strategy for keeping an individual foremost in mind. This approach to instructional management is a flexible structure within which creative innovation can take place. "In the case of media there is accumulating evidence that each individual appears to have a style which enables him to learn best from a class of media."[30] Differential grouping coupled with child-selection of learning media frees the child to learn as an individual.

Differential grouping depends upon synergistic action. (See Figure 5.) This continuing professional decision process illustrates the pivotal role of a classroom teacher. Successful or ineffective learning experiences depend upon the quality of cooperative planning. Likewise, the best plans may be of little value, because differential grouping has not been a component of instructional management. Opportunities for an individual child to learn can be eclipsed by inadequate grouping rather than by insufficient preparation. The "teachable moment" is one when the most interest exists; a media program must provide a range of resources on a variety of subjects to meet as many of these situations as possible.[31] Thus, differential grouping for individualized instruction functions as the follow-through component of synergistic action.

Control: A Daily Evaluation Function

Discipline has become a major problem for many teachers. To begin with, *discipline* has traditionally meant superimposed control by an authority figure. Whenever such a condition exists, the ifs and don'ts rule

---

[30] W. C. Meierhenry, "National Media Standards for Planning and Teaching," *American Library Association Bulletin*, Vol. 63 (February, 1969), p. 238.
[31] *Ibid.*, p. 239.

by virtue of threat of punishment. Hence, work and learning behavior take place in a negative environment, and a child conforms to the punitive teacher.

In contrast, the ultimate objective is to have a child develop self-control. This process is one in which an individual child gradually becomes an independent adult who is capable of interacting with others in socially acceptable ways. Collier and others suggest that a criterion to judge effective classroom control is ". . . not how quiet the children are or how rapidly they respond to teacher commands, but how well they develop toward self-control."[32]

Each day that a classroom teacher exhibits a positive working relationship with children, and that his observable behavior and judgment are considered consistently fair by the learners, he has a better chance to foster self-control among the children. Punishment with discretion, infrequently administered, should be the behavioral response of teachers. Behavioral problems usually have many sources, including a teacher's inconsistent and punitive approach to pupil control. Other sources which contribute to behavioral problems may be instructional management and curriculum experiences. Good classroom control requires daily evaluation of the total school experiences. A teacher should seek reasons for misbehavior rather than reacting harshly. When living-learning experiences are relevant to an individual child, self-control is a continuous behavioral response and misbehavior diminishes markedly.

Sharing Management Responsibility

Management of learning experiences is a shared responsibility between pupil and teacher.[33] Sharing management responsibilities with the learner enables the child to perceive his own worthiness. This is consistent with the guidance function. Accurate diagnoses of maturity level and academic competence allow valid judgments to be made with reference to the type and amount a child, small group, or whole class should be involved in decision making. Too often, the extent of pupil involvement in the decision-making process is one of the two extremes: either the pupils passively respond to teacher commands, or the teacher adapts

---

[32] Calhoun C. Collier, et. al., *Teaching in the Modern Elementary School* (New York: The Macmillan Company, 1967), p. 216.

[33] Sharing management responsibility in the elementary school with its constituents is a primary factor in creating and maintaining pupil control. Pupil involvement in appropriate decisions provides a child with an opportunity to identify on a personalized basis with living-learning experiences.

an attitude of laissez-faire and the students rule the classroom. Each of these behavioral responses prevents development of academic integrity and self-control. Again, methodical orientation to problem solving that is skillfully phased into the curriculum can give an individual child, small group, or whole class a comprehended foundation upon which knowledgeable decisions can be made. It is important to remember that the abilities to share and to be responsible, which are required by society, are learned behavioral responses. Passive learning cannot any longer characterize the beginning years of supervised learning. There is a social mandate for shared management of learning experiences within the elementary school curriculum.

UTILIZATION OF AUXILIARY PERSONNEL

Individualized Instruction a Shared Responsibility

Irrespective of curriculum organization, supplementary and auxiliary personnel have become accepted within the total operation of the elementary school. At one time, the classroom teacher and the building principal together assumed an omnibus role for which they were not qualified, especially in the realm of evaluation. Today the educational evaluation of an individual child's academic and social needs and his general welfare take into consideration the professional judgments of personnel involved who may include an elementary school counselor, psychologist, social worker, physician, parents, members of community agencies, and industrial workers.

Professional Assistants   For some time now, curriculum area specialists have cooperated with classroom teachers in curriculum planning and evaluation; including supplementary service personnel in the evaluative diagnosis of pupil change is also becoming more generally accepted among educators. The *case conference* approach to pupil evaluation is now fundamental in providing for individual differentiation. The use of supplementary personnel service manifests itself in the fact that classroom teachers and building principals no longer attempt to be "all things to all children."

Community Agencies   Heretofore, community agencies have been peripheral in education. By including community agencies in living-learning experiences of children, the learning process becomes an integrated community effort. In the past, the personnel and services of community agencies have been used for field trips and for rehabilitation purposes.

Prevention has become the focus of guidance. Community agencies can make a valuable and far-reaching contribution to the learning process.

Paraprofessional Assistance   Auxiliary personnel have been added to the growing educational team. In contrast to the professional diagnostic role played by supplementary service personnel, *paraprofessionals* have a supporting role; they work with the individual classroom teacher. In the past, auxiliary persons have been accepted with mixed feelings by teachers. Their reactions have ranged from full acceptance to resentment of intrusion. The latter is usually felt by less professionally secure classroom teachers and principals.

This innovation in elementary school operation, like any other, requires in-service programming for both local school faculties and auxiliary helpers. Fundamentally, these in-service programs must inculcate in auxiliary helpers an understanding that their responsibilities are supportive to the professional's supervision of direct living-learning instructional sequences.

Job Descriptions   A principal should have a policy statement from his superiors with regard to employment and use of paraprofessional assistants, and agreement should be reached concerning the specific activities that are acceptable for a paraprofessional within the on-going educational program. Kopp suggests seven qualifications to be considered when initiating a program that incorporates auxiliary helpers into any elementary school system. These qualifications are: adequate assessment of need, delineation of principal's concern, readiness of the board of education, readiness of the professional, clarification of defined limits, articulation of supervision, evaluation, and projected concern for the future.[34]

In-Service Study   Preparing the professional is primary to successful utilization of auxiliary personnel in the elementary school program. Kopp

---

[34] O. W. Kopp, "Hiring, Training, Using Teacher Aides in Elementary Schools," *Elementary Principal's Letter* (Supplementary No. 1), 1968. The following is a list of acceptable activities for auxiliary personnel and those which seem to overstep reasonable bounds. *Acceptable Activities:* "preparing duplicated materials; handling routine reports; collecting money; making routine phone calls; running errands; compiling attendance information; picking up library books; setting up audio-visual aids; assisting with cafeteria, lavatory, and corridor supervision; assisting young children with clothing." *Not Acceptable Activities:* "serving as a substitute teacher in case of illness of the professional; 'assisting' the individual child who needs special help in reading or other work; 'teaching' small groups of children who need special help or who are working on a special project; 'hearing' groups read; disciplining or striking a child who misbehaves; assuming full responsibility in a cafeteria, auditorium, playground, or classroom; conducting a parent conference; writing reports to parents."

provides functional guidelines for principal leadership in preparing for the use of auxiliary personnel. He writes:

> The principal who plans to use teacher aides, lay readers, or library aides should take concrete steps to prepare the professional staff to make the best possible use of nonprofessional help. Principal and faculty should reach an understanding that auxiliary helpers: (1) "*Cannot* and *should not* assume responsibility for teaching. Hearing children read is an example of a teaching practice. Duplicating work for teachers is a clear-cut auxiliary service. (2) *Cannot* be exploited or ignored by the professional staff. They must receive support from the staff to do their jobs and be helpful to the teachers. (3) *Will* make mistakes. They will need help, not criticism. (4) *Will* lack confidence at first and that staff members can help them feel secure on the job. (5) *Should not* be left alone to supervise children. (6) *Are not* licensed teachers. Rather, they are employed to make the teaching act more effective—not easier. (7) *Can* promote friends for the school, if their experience is a pleasant one, because they represent the community—they live in it.[35]

Conversely, the auxiliary personnel must understand their role and range of responsibility. Thus, they should realize that supervision is essential. Kopp continues, "The fundamental aim of supervision is to help employees do a better job. Thus, supervision and evaluation of performance are inseparable. Auxiliary workers should understand this. When done tactfully, supervision will not be considered a threat."[36]

Kopp concludes by stating: "The investment of time and effort in supervising and directing the efforts of auxiliary personnel will result in more effective use of nonprofessional personnel. This in turn should help the principal provide pupils with a better education and teachers with more opportunity to teach, plan, and use their professional skills for professional tasks."[37]

SUMMARY

An elementary school guidance program that emphasizes synergistic action and utilizes the resources of an instructional media center to

---

[35] *Ibid.*

[36] *Ibid.* Factors to be considered in supervisory conferences are: "direct professional observation; written observation data; children's reactions; teacher reactions; parent reactions; check sheet evaluation (check sheet to be developed cooperatively by professional and auxiliary helpers)."

[37] *Ibid.*

personalize learning serves as a flexible foundation to create a functional approach to individualized instruction. Within this instructional format, living-learning experiences are pupil-centered. This approach to learning allows a child to emerge from the elementary school as a self-controlled independent learner. The ever-present challenge for contemporary classroom teachers is to expertly manage pupil-centered decentralized learning experiences and utilize auxiliary personnel in such a manner that the teachers have more time to plan and participate in professional tasks.

Major Themes

1. Elementary school guidance is ubiquitous.

2. In the past, data have been gathered about problems of an individual child, but the child seldom received benefit from this knowledge in the form of prescribed assistance.

3. Each classroom teacher is the key to effective elementary guidance in living-learning experiences for children.

4. Synergistic action is recommended over independent action as a means of diagnosing academic, social, and clinical needs of an individual child.

5. The instructional materials center (IMC) has become the nerve center for personalized learning and individualized instruction.

6. Creative inquiry has become the central focus of personalized learning.

7. Creative inquiry, self-discipline, intellectual honesty, and the capacity to think clearly are desirable outcomes which result from making an IMC the nerve center for learning at the elementary school level.

8. An IMC serves as a planning and learning center for both children and teachers.

9. Utilization of the IMC fosters learning independence and as a result provides for quality education on a mass scale.

10. Many teachers will have to reorient themselves in order to manage pupil-centered decentralized learning experiences.

11. Pupil-oriented learning experiences accentuate both guidance and independent learning.

12. Differential grouping as a component to decentralized learning management is fundamental to individualized instruction.

13. Emphasis should be placed upon assisting a child to acquire increasing self-control rather than to respond to teacher commands.

14. Management of learning experiences should be a shared responsibility as a natural outgrowth of pupil–teacher planning.

15. Auxiliary personnel and services in consonance with paraprofessional assistants, when professionally accepted and supervised, give teachers more opportunity to teach, plan, and use their professional skills for professional tasks.

SUPPLEMENTARY READINGS

Abraham, Willard, A *Time for Teaching* (New York: Harper and Row, 1964).

Anderson, Ralph A., "Open Learning Places," *Educational Technology*, Vol. 10 (June, 1970), pp. 13–15.

Becker, Harry A., *Working With Teacher Aides*, Croft Leadership Folio No. 7 (New London, Conn.: Crofts Educational Services, 1968).

Blaker, Kenneth E. and R. W. Bennet, "Behavioral Counseling for Elementary School Children," *Elementary School Journal*, Vol. 70 (May, 1970), pp. 411–17.

Byrne, Richard Hill, "For Elementary Schools: A Human Development Specialist," *Educational Leadership*, Vol. XXIV (January, 1967), pp. 349–55.

Cottingham, Harold F., "Guidance Function in the Elementary School," *The Personnel and Guidance Journal*, Vol. XXXI (April, 1953), pp. 453–54.

———, "The Unique Characteristics of Elementary Guidance," *Education*, Vol. LXXIII (April, 1953), pp. 508–9.

Dinkmeyer, Don, "Elementary School Guidance and the Classroom Teacher," *Elementary School Guidance and Counseling*, Vol. I (1967), pp. 15–26.

_____, "When Guidance and Curriculum Collaborate," *Educational Leadership*, Vol. XXV (February, 1968), pp. 443–48.

Dreikurs, R., *Psychology in the Classroom*, 2nd ed. (New York: Harper and Row, 1968).

Glovinsky, A., J. P. Johns, J. E. Keefe, and L. G. Lanza, "Paraprofessionals," *School Management*, Vol. 13 (February, 1969), pp. 46–50ff.

Hellerich, R. L., "Creative Learning Center," *Elementary School Journal*, Vol. 69 (February, 1969), pp. 259–64.

Hornburger, Jane M., "Working With Teacher Aides," *Catholic School Journal* (January, 1968), pp. 34–35.

Howe, M. J. A., "Positive Reinforcement: A Humanizing Approach to Teacher Control in the Classroom," *National Elementary Principal*, Vol. 49 (April, 1970), pp. 31–34.

Johnson, W. G., "Utilizing Teacher Aides," *Clearing House* (December, 1967), pp. 229–33.

King, J. C., "What Behavioral Research Has Meant to the Practitioner," *National Elementary Principal*, Vol. 49 (May, 1970), pp. 55–58.

Lampman, L., "Library into Learning Center," *Instructor*, Vol. 79 (June, 1970), pp. 27–28.

Lee, Dorris M., *Diagnostic Teaching* (Washington, D.C.: National Education Association, Department of Elementary, Kindergarten and Nursery Education, 1966).

Like, D. W., "More on Learning Resource Centers," *Childhood Education*, Vol. 46 (January, 1970), pp. 209–12.

McCandless, B. R., *Children*, 3rd ed. (New York: Holt, Rinehart and Winston, Inc., 1967).

McNeff, Marie O., "Analysis of Services Provided by School Counselors in Selected Midwestern Elementary Schools" (Ed. D. dissertation, University of Nebraska, 1967).

Mattick, William E. and N. A. Nickolas, "A Team Approach to Guidance," *The Personnel and Guidance Journal*, Vol. XLIV (May, 1964), pp. 922–24.

Moody, F. B. and T. J. Rookey, "How to Pigeonhole Teacher Aides for Better Performance and Production: NEA and Pennsylvania State Studies," *American School Board Journal*, Vol. 156 (September, 1968), pp. 26–28.

National Education Association Research Division, "How the Profession Feels About Teacher Aides, *NEA Journal* (November, 1967), pp. 16–17.

————, "How Teacher Aides Feel About Their Jobs," *NEA Journal* (November, 1967), pp. 17–19.

Pellegreno, D. D., "Elementary School Counselor and the Affective Domain," *Elementary School Guidance and Counseling*, Vol. 4 (May, 1970), pp. 253–59.

Quinn, Paul R., "Common Misconceptions in Guidance," *Education*, Vol. LXXXVII (January, 1967), pp. 277–82.

Rapport, Virginia, and Mary N. S. W. Parker, *Learning Centers: Children on Their Own* (Washington, D.C.: The Association for Childhood Education International, 1970.)

Smith, Hyrum M., "Preventing Difficulties Through Guidance," *Education*, Vol. LXXXIII (January, 1963), pp. 266–69.

"Using Auxiliary Personnel: Study by the Bank Street College of Education, New York," *Michigan Educational Journal*, Vol. 45 (April, 1968), p. 29.

Weisz, Vera C., "Becoming Teacher Aides for Young Children," *Childhood Education* (December, 1967), pp. 256–57.

Willey, Roy DeVerl, and Melvin Dunn, *The Role of the Teacher in the Guidance Program* (Bloomington, Ill.: McKnight and McKnight Pub. Co., 1964).

6

LEADERSHIP ESSENTIAL TO IMPLEMENTING INNOVATION

INSTRUCTIONAL TEAM

Organizational Sets Over the Years

The twenty-first century promises to be an extension of education's "golden age" which began in the 1950's. However, curriculum for the future will depend upon how well planning is addressed by leadership to educational demands yet to be programmed. Stavisky developed assumptions around anticipated educational demands which call for the interplay of programming, equipment, and facilities.[1] With all this innovation, the traditional school fades into history as a crude relic to be viewed in the archives of education with a sense of wonder.

It is anticipated that in the next century the school will become a comprehensive unit combining all educational endeavours to form a large community center, housing many learning stations or zones to meet the demand for knowledge on the part of anyone—from the

---

[1] Leonard Price Stavisky, "New Directions in Education," from *The School of Tomorrow*, Copyright, ©, 1964 by Macfadden-Bartell Corporation and International Fair Consultants, Inc. Used by permission of the publisher. The basic assumptions are: "1) that mankind will ultimately resolve the conflicts between automation and employment; 2) that the shorter workweek will strengthen family ties through joint participation in cultural and recreational activities; 3) that education in the year 2,000 will be a lifetime experience and that all age groups will go to school; 4) that men and women in every business and profession will require constant retraining in order to keep abreast of the dynamics of research and development; 5) that a technological revolution will accelerate standards of excellence through the availability of vast, untapped depositories of learning resources and instructional media."

preschooler to the octogenarian. Direct dial computers will be common-place, and individualized self-directed study will be the instructional mode. Demonstration centers and television will be primary units of communication systems supporting the learning process. The most amazing innovation may very well be the "studysphere." A six-foot opaque spheroid connected with all types of communication systems will provide instant contact with the great minds of his time for the learner—who will not have to leave his home.[2]

Whenever new technological media are suggested, many professionals cry, "Machines will replace the teacher!" Nothing could be farther from reality. At last, curriculum planners recognize that communications systems can provide the teacher with more diverse information than any teacher could amass by himself in a lifetime. By programming instruc-tion and providing systematic guidance and evaluation for a student, the design of personalized curriculum remains a function of the indi-vidual teacher. No matter how sophisticated the technical media placed within a school system to enhance learning, the effectiveness still de-pends on the quality of direction by the professional faculty. However, increasing inclusion of technological media in the schools does suggest that teachers at all levels, from pre-school to graduate school, should survey their professional roles carefully and teach themselves to use more advanced instructional methods. From self-contained classrooms to team teaching, to team coordinator, the teacher of tomorrow will have to lead by arming himself with electronic equipment. Supported by auxiliary personnel, he should be able to create individual instructional sequences. Electronic equipment can be a help to learning rather than a hindrance.[3]

With the change in classroom teachers' professional role and the in-creased emphasis upon individualization of instruction, ten trends have been identified by Gores which seem to portray the character of to-morrow's school. (See Figure 6.) Analysis of these trends shows that their elements are already operational in more affluent communities, to the point of involving computerized data processing. First, it is antici-pated that the teacher-centered classroom will disappear; that as a coordinator of learning experiences, a teacher will assist pupils in the self-education process. Second, schools built about an instructional materials

---

[2] *Ibid.*, p. 16.

[3] *Ibid.*, p. 17. "The teacher of tomorrow will be called upon to provide personalized guidance in depth, to program the instructional sequence, to evaluate the student's effort in relation to background, aptitude, goals, skills, and achievement, and to be-come familiar with a seemingly awesome battery of electronic devices which eventu-ally will become increasingly simple to operate."

FIGURE 6
School Trends

FROM: School of Today	TO: School of Tomorrow
1. Organized for groups of children	Organized for the self-educating individual
2. The self-contained school	The self-contained school
3. Teaching to transmit facts	Teaching to inculcate values
4. Teacher as general practitioner	Teacher as specialist educational counselor
5. Education as a separate community service	Education as a subsystem of total community services
6. The schoolhouse as an isolated unit in a school system	The school house as a connected unit in a national and international network of communication
7. School systems organized as elementary, junior high, and senior high schools	Schools organized as ungraded primary, middle, high school, and community college
8. Schools operating 1,000 hours a year	Schools operating at least 4,000 hours a year
9. Financial support mostly from local real estate	Financial support mostly state and federal
10. Buildings designed for indestructibility and antisepsis	Buildings designed for performance and beauty

Source: "The School of Tomorrow—Ten Trends," by Harold B. Gores, from *The School of Tomorrow*, Copyright, ©, 1964 by Macfadden-Bartell Corporation and International Fair Consultants, Inc. Used by permission of the publisher.

center (IMC) with flexible arrangements will allow for maximum utilization of space and resources. Third, a major breakthrough should occur in placing emphasis upon the teaching of values and processes rather than dispensing facts. Thus, the school will become a place where there is a lateral transmission of knowledge in its broadest sense in the community context. Learning will take on a new meaning, relevant to purposeful living. Fourth, there is a trend toward specialization and increased knowledge and counseling. Even with academic specialization, the elementary school specialist should first have expertise in reading, supplemented by academic competencies in many different areas. By the end of the twentieth century, the function of guidance should be generally accepted by teachers of elementary school children. Fifth, as the elementary school has always been organized on the concept of neighborhoods, schools of tomorrow may include learners from preschool children to retired adults. It may become, as Gores suggests, a subsystem of a total community. Sixth, the most challenging possibility lies in the instant international communication systems with which a school of tomorrow will be connected. The world then would become as close as turning some dials and switches. No longer is local knowledge of a community or regional orientation sufficient; there is a mandate to be aware of and knowledgeable about world cultures. Thus, communications media promise to make intercultural attitudes a reality. Next, changes in administrative units will occur. The significant element probably will be an attempt to group children that have similar developmental needs. This trend is illustrated by the emergence of the middle school during the past decade. Continuous progress from preschool learning through college and graduate school may also be accepted as a natural process. Eighth, with knowledge as a primary tool for positive participation in citizenship, the nine-month school should eventually come to an end. As a community center for learning, a school of tomorrow can be expected to be operated twelve months a year, serving young and old who are ready and able to learn. Ninth, additional financial support will have to be forthcoming from state and federal governments if the present standards are to be maintained, let alone improved. Each year an increasing number of school budgets are being voted down because local real estate taxes have approached a saturation point, and the public is increasingly unwilling to assume tax increases to support public and private education. Finally, school design will reflect the functional flexibility necessary to implement curriculum innovation. Yesterday's schools are dysfunctional in tomorrow's dynamic educational world.

Tomorrow's schools will reflect the expansion of those trends that began in the past decades. However, as today's school faculty concerns itself with excellence in studies, the curriculum in tomorrow's school should be able to extend that concern to include excellence in living. Carr pointedly describes American education as "opportunity, quality, freedom, and diversity."[4] These same characteristics are the cornerstones of the traditional "good life."

---

[4] William G. Carr, "Characteristics of American Education," in *The School of Tomorrow, op. cit.,* pp. 45–49.

Functional Building Design

A rationale for an evolution in functional building design and resource utilization may be based on a team instructional approach to learning that is consistent with learning theory, improved technology, and guidance. A survey of school buildings and curriculum organization shows that the elementary school generalist, working alone, seldom utilized physical and educational resources to the maximum. Today the stockpiling of knowledge renders the elementary generalist obsolete along with the traditional elementary school building.

School buildings are becoming more than a place to house children. From one-room buildings with creosoted floors, immovable seats, wood stove heating, and poor lighting, they are evolving into air-conditioned, esthetically pleasing, functional learning centers. Within this century, schools have been, and in some cases continue to be, erected for those who have passed; few were built with a concern for the present and in anticipation of the future. Hence, they became at once dysfunctional monuments to the past.

During the twentieth century, the speed of change and interplay of human events have greatly affected school building programs throughout the nation. Little significant school building occurred during the first two decades of this century; however, during the 1930's, schools were erected under the auspices of the CCC at a fraction of their present replacement cost.[5] But this building was done at a time when educational innovation was not a dynamic force and the school population was comparatively small. Demographic shifts had not yet caused urban centers to spill out into suburbia; strip cities were still a phenomenon of the future.

Entry into World War II halted domestic building. After the war, a severe shortage of classrooms became evident as children flooded existing schools to overflowing. In turn, enlarged faculty and facilities became critical requirements as the tide of students swept into both elementary and secondary schools. Consequently, the school building boom of the 1950's exploded in full force.

Heretofore, planning a school building had been primarily an administrative function. Teachers, supervisors, and area specialists were seldom asked to participate in planning sessions. Today, however, new buildings are the result of a team approach which includes the professional faculty as well as community personnel in establishing educational ob-

---

[5] The CCC is the Civil Conservation Corps, an agency of the New Deal which provided work for the unemployed youth of the nation.

jectives for new building and determining the educational and social expectations of the community. School structures are now being built from a base of professional involvement and community participation, rather than being erected to store children with little regard for the curricula to be undertaken within their walls.

Schools today have abruptly departed from traditional concepts of school design. (See Figure 7.) One such school, the Lewis and Clark Elementary School, Riverview Gardens School District, St. Louis, Missouri, incorporates these significant technological innovations which affect curriculum development and the team teaching approach to learning: 1) the unusual design of a snail, 2) a perception core, 3) an internal stream aquarium, 4) the absence of inside walls, 5) a children's theater, 6) a satellite kitchen, 7) a shelter for physical education, 8) the "nerve center"—an instructional materials center, 9) a soft floor covering, and 10) air conditioning.[6] These inclusions did not just happen. They arose "naturally and organically out of a new sort of program conceived and planned by the community."[7] The Lewis and Clark Elementary School does illustrate a trend to incorporate the best of technology and advanced curricula in a school designed for the education of children in the closing decades of this century.

Looking into the twenty-first century, team instruction and planning as a mode of operation requires expanded facilities. That these facilities must expand in increasingly less space is a fact that must be contended with daily. Wiedersum and Wiedersum envision a school containing a multi-unit base complimented by towers in an interconnected cluster of supporting circular multi-storied modular floor units.[8] As a community learning center, this total concept of education is electronics–oriented. This center is open 24 hours a day; it provides for interrelationship between departments, yet preserves their individuality; and by vertical expansion it allows for additions and flexible reorganization.[9] This construction concept provides for continual updating as change comes about in design of curriculum and methodology. The school of tomorrow promises to be a total community commitment to education, where

---

[6] Educational Facilities Laboratories, Southeastern Regional Center, University of Tennessee, *Profile of a Significant School* (February, 1964), p. 4. Copies can be secured from Director, School Planning Laboratory, University of Tennessee, Knoxville, Tennessee.

[7] *Ibid.*

[8] Norman J. Wiedersum and Frederic G. Wiedersum, "Designing the School for Tomorrow," in *The School of Tomorrow* (New York: Macfadden-Bartell Corporation, 1964), pp. 26–35.

[9] *Ibid.*

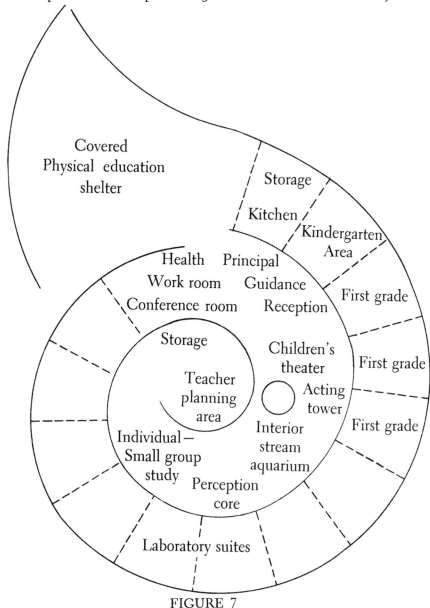

FIGURE 7
Profile of a Significant School
Riverview Gardens Elementary Schools, St. Louis, Missouri

Source: Educational Facilities Laboratories, Southeastern Regional Center, University of Tennessee, *Profile of a Significant School* (February, 1964), pp. 8–9.

the education of an individual is a lifetime activity under the supervision of an instructional team.

The Role of the Instructional Team

Hutchins writes, "The aim of American education in an age of rapid change should be to do what it can to help everybody gain complete possession of all his powers. As John Dewey says, this is the only possible aim. It is now clear that the only thing we can do is what we ought to have been doing all along."[10] An instructional team, as individual members or as a cooperative unit, seeks ways to meet this commitment, beginning at the elementary school level. Inherent within Dewey's single aim of education appears to be a human problem which Newman mentions: "At no time have educators in this country hypothesized that the purpose of education is for the joy of learning and a richer sense of self, instead of for practical material purposes or for high moral purposes."[11]

The instructional team should come to grips with the fact that many of the present day curricular alternatives are highly structured and may literally inhibit learning. At the same time, for culturally disadvantaged learners, their curriculum content may be totally irrelevant to their backgrounds. Therefore, as individuals and as a cooperative unit, elementary school instructional teams should exercise leadership within the parameters of daily instruction. Unlike the dramatic leadership of the political arena, an instructional team member exercises humanistic leadership which is manifested in his observable behavior and is interpreted by both the learner and his parents.

Accepting Dewey's single aim for education, the effect of an elementary school instructional team's leadership is the individual child's positive contribution as an adult citizen. The instructional team should never forget that classroom management, personal behavior, genuine curiosity, and observable professional consistency are all part of effective short- and long-range leadership. The total impact of this disciplined dedication often is an inspiration to the learner, enhancing the possibility for creation of affirmative attitudes toward self, which in turn can raise the individual's potential level of aspiration for personal excellence.

Flexible Scheduling   When an instructional team combines individualized instruction, technology, and humanistic behavior in the classroom, their leadership can then be extended through innovative management of the time within a single day. A new and exciting breakthrough in

---

10 Robert M. Hutchins, "Permanence and Change," *The Center Magazine*, Vol. I, No. 6 (September, 1969), p. 6.

11 Ruth G. Newman, "How American Education Got That Way," *Psychiatry and Social Science Review*, Vol. III, No. 5 (May, 1969), p. 18.

time management is flexible scheduling of *modules*, a radical departure from the graded classroom and fixed scheduling. Utilizing a basis of requested time, some classes could be as short as fifteen minutes or as long as more than one hour. All classes might not meet every day. This system allows for individual instruction, and (if room is available) for the accommodation of many small groups with up to and over one hundred children. This pattern is usually associated with subject matter specialization; however, it could be modified to add another flexible dimension to a continuous progress structure.

Flexible modular scheduling has increasing appeal for both teachers and pupils. On the one hand, teachers have more time to plan and meet with smaller instructional groups; on the other hand, pupils are given more opportunity for responsible behavior during their unscheduled modules, which are set aside for independent or team learning experiences. Also, the same teacher can motivate learning and teach better under these conditions.

Another striking advantage of this system is its aid to rapid diagnosis. By continually varying time allotments and class size for teacher-led presentations, a teacher may be able to recognize learning strengths and limitations sooner. Within the framework of modular scheduling, a higher degree of objective evaluation of an individual child should be an outgrowth of coordinated instructional practice.

Considering the assimilated advances made during the past two decades in learning theory, methodology, and media utilization, an instructional team is armed now with the means to increase both the objective quality and type of evaluation on a personal basis. Objectivity increases when the following ingredients are present: 1) competent teaching, 2) reasonable class size, 3) adequate instructional materials, software/hardware, 4) enlightened supervision, 5) a Board of Education that is leadership-oriented. (See Figure 8, p. 94.)

Coupled with the guidance function and the use of auxiliary personnel, a modular system releases living-learning experiences from the traditional time structure and increases the probability for one-to-one contact with an individual child. This increase in personal relationships between the learner and the instructional team makes diagnosis and programming for educational need more objectively efficient by shortening the time lapse between data gathering and synergistic action. Flexible modular scheduling lends itself to team teaching and technological innovation.[12] Hence, as an instructional curriculum pattern, it represents a genuine innovation for the benefit of the individual learner.

---

[12] Catherine Watson, "School Officials Find Modular Scheduling Works," *Minneapolis Tribune*, June 23, 1968, p. B-6.

Check Points

✔ Competent teaching

✔ Reasonable class size

✔ Adequate instructional materials
   "Software/Hardware"

✔ Enlightened supervision

✔ Board of Education—
   Leadership-oriented.

FIGURE 8

Ingredients of a Good Teaching/Learning Situation

PUBLIC RELATIONS AND COMMUNITY SUPPORT

Public Understanding and Community Support

Public relations programs are essential to effective daily operation of any school system. Kindred describes school public relations as "a process of communication between the school and community for the purpose of increasing citizen understanding of educational needs and practices and encouraging intelligent citizen interest and cooperation in the work of improving the school.[13]

---

[13] Leslie W. Kindred, *School Public Relations* (Englewood Cliffs, N.J.: Prentice-Hall, Inc., 1963), p. 16. "Stated somewhat differently, school public relations is a combination of the following ideas and practices: 1) A way of life expressed daily by each person on the school staff in his relations with other staff members, pupils, parents, its program, problems, and accomplishments—in short—good human rela-

Accepting Kindred's definition of school public relations, his eight objectives serve as criteria with which to evaluate the effectiveness of a public relations program. The objectives are:

> 1) To develop intelligent understanding of the school in all aspects of its operation; 2) To determine how the public feels about the school and what it wishes the school to accomplish; 3) To secure adequate financial support for a sound educational program; 4) To help citizens feel a more direct responsibility for the quality of education the school provides; 5) To earn the school good will, respect, and confidence of the public in professional personnel and services of the institution; 6) To bring about public realization of the need for change and what must be done to facilitate essential progress; 7) To involve citizens in the work of the school and the solving of educational problems; 8) To promote a genuine spirit of cooperation between the school and community in sharing leadership for the improvement of community life.[14]

Over the years, worthy innovative practices have been curtailed and even voted down because a public relations program was not an integral part of the local school faculty's on-going activity. Consistent with a mirror image, where a school program reflects parents' concerns at any given time, the quality and intelligent incidence of community involvement serves to sustain the local school program. Educators must continually be reminded of the fact that the instructional team can effect long-range change when their innovations are understood by the public. Therefore, a school public relations program becomes a catalytic agent which can be an extralegal force in continual support for coordinated innovative programming.

The Public Relations Program

To suggest that some type of public school public relations program did not exist at the local level would be unfair. However, the public relations effort of most professional faculties is limited both in scope and consistency. Unfortunately, information about local school programs often is not systematically disseminated. Very often the Parent–Teachers As-

---

tions. 2) A systematic, honest, and continuing series of activities for educating people in the community to the purposes of the school, its program, problems, and accomplishments. 3) A systematic, honest, and continuing series of activities for finding out what people in the community think about their schools and what they want their schools to provide for children. 4) An active partnership between the school and community, in which professional educators and laymen work together for essential modification and improvements in the educational program."

[14] *Ibid.*, pp. 16–17.

sociation, school newspaper, periodic open houses, and parent–teacher conferences are the usual means of informing the community, thus neglecting a large sector of potential support: single persons and those married persons with no children or with children no longer in school.

Faculty behavior, at times, does much to inform the public about the school. Regrettably, teacher morale may be low; teachers in organized groups have recently become increasingly militant. Kindred points out that a high level of teacher morale can not be maintained in an "atmosphere of rigid economy and public indifference to the importance of their services."[15] He continues, "As matters now stand, the income of a high percentage are below those received by skilled and unskilled labor."[16] The mass media have indeed helped to bring national strife in education to the forefront. In retrospect, if consistent and systematic school public relations programs that each sought to provide an "honest" appraisal of local needs had been initiated long ago, the funds required to maintain, modify, and extend programming might have been forthcoming. Educators need to remember that financial backing for new programs is provided only when those who pay the bill clearly understand the intent and anticipated outcome with respect to improving education for children of the community.

Activities—Old and New   School public relations programs become ineffective when there is an overreliance upon a single form of communication or when the community believes that it is being asked to participate in insignificant activities. Relevant activities, varied in format, energize the public into self-propelling action. In many schools, public relations activities remain dominated by an elite core who do not attempt to broaden the base for greater involvement.

Basic to effective public relations is variety of means of involvement in the pursuit of understanding the local operation of a school. Meticulous advance planning which is consistent with established educational objectives provides a foundation for a school public relations program. Some of the seldom–used ways a community can be consistently informed are 1) have weekly seminars explaining and demonstrating materials and methods utilized in newly initiated programs; 2) organize evening or weekend workshops where simulation materials are utilized for the purpose of assisting the lay public in becoming acquainted with the many and complex decisions that must be made by every instructional team; 3) sponsor field trips which provide the lay community with the opportunity to observe and inquire about proposed innovations prior to local adoption; 4) have panel discussions composed of students as

---

15 *Ibid.*, p. 30.
16 *Ibid.*

well as faculty members in order to include *total* community in the program; 5) invite unusual guest speakers such as members of the state legislature who serve on the education committee to acquire a comprehensive view of educational need, not only on the local level but statewide; 6) involve interested lay persons as observers and resource persons when curriculum planning is undertaken; 7) through news media, consistently inform the public of pupil and faculty achievement as well as of program modification within the original intent; 8) from time to time, provide local television community service time for an education spectacular or for short highlight news spots (five to ten minutes) once a week where different subjects are presented, thus reaching an ever–increasing number of viewers; 9) have *adult and continuing education programs* which provide an opportunity for large segments of the community to closely identify with the school, its problems, and needs. Consistent school public relations programming is a primary prerequisite for successful education, regardless of district size or location. A combination of traditional means and these new ways to involve the community can enhance the total community's continual support for local educational programs.

Value of Public Relations Programs

Because of many uncontrollable external pressures,[17] sufficient funds for innovation are often hard to obtain. This problem is complicated because many faculty members would rather continue the status quo than fight for change. However, even though a school public relations program may demand a great amount of faculty participation, including a public relations specialist, the effort continues to reap dividends. When educational programming becomes an understood community enterprise resulting from a consistent public school relations program, support of continued innovation will follow. As the school program becomes detached from the community, curtailment of programs is an omnipresent threat. The rewards of meaningful school public relations can be consistent pride in and ideological and financial support of local schools.

SYSTEMATIC EVALUATION AND MODIFICATION

Evaluation: Short– and Long–Term Objectives

Each aspect of a school's objective *evaluation* provides a basis from which to make realistic modifications of existing programs. Honest

---

[17] See above, pp. 37-38.

appraisal of educational programming must be in terms of the local school faculty's educational objectives. Evaluation should be a systematic and on-going activity if the accumulated data is to have any impact on current situations and planning for the future.

As an on-going activity, program appraisal should be viewed as a multilevel function, divided into *short– and long–term evaluations.* Short-term evaluation usually coincides with immediate needs and/or primary objectives. Simultaneously, short-term results should be analyzed in terms of a logical sequence which supports long-range anticipation. In the past, faculties regarded evaluation as an activity relating only to periodic issuance of report cards to parents. Recently, however, far-sighted administrative leaders have recognized the need for "total" accountability in order to maintain and increase community support of educational programming.

Appropriate Evaluation Devices

Assuming that individualized instruction and nongradedness are accepted as concepts of educational operation at the local level, evaluative devices and subsequent interpretation of data for the purpose of evaluation must be appropriate for the initiated programs. If a child is accepted as an individual, inclusive of his learning capability, then programs can be designed specifically for him. This means that national norms, often used as measures for success and pass/failure, may have to be interpreted in a different way. Evaluative devices should be created for the local learner according to local resources.

Nongradedness and individualized instruction implies that the learner's self-concept and attitudes toward learning are important factors in evaluation. Those who initiate such programs continually need to keep in mind that time is needed to redevelop affirmative attitudes, and that in a time of transition, progress may not be readily apparent. Both the learner and teacher must adjust to new approaches to learning.

When team teaching and guidance are coupled with nongradedness and individualized instruction, evaluation takes on new dimensions. In the recent past paper tests, report cards, and parent-teacher conferences were the common practices in evaluation. Some of the newer techniques utilized by elementary school personnel are 1) case conference analysis, 2) sociograms which assist in gaining insight into group and class structure, 3) interest and attitude inventories for curriculum development and modification, 4) anecdotal records which provide knowledge of behavioral patterns, 5) skill checklists which record skill competency and the date when demonstrated successfully, and 6) increased participation in diagnosis by specialists such as the psychologist, medical doctor, nurse-teacher, and elementary guidance counselor who acts as liasion within this matrix of professional diagnosticians. Another helpful way that evaluation assists in rapid diagnosis is by keeping pertinent data in a cumulative record for each child in the attendance unit. This information provides invaluable assistance for those attendance units receiving transfer pupils.

In the school of tomorrow, evaluation will be a continual system of diagnosis and creation of programs of study for individual children. Excellence remains a primary goal for education; however, modification of and creating learning environments for a child are fundamental concerns before excellence can be a realistically expected outcome. Hence, evaluation devices for innovative curricula must be specifically designed to measure intended behavioral outcomes in terms of educational objectives at the local attendance unit level.

Data as an Index for Modification As in the continuous cycle of data gathering characteristic of many elementary school guidance programs, analyzed evaluation data of school educational programs have to be translated into observable action. Too often, innovative programs are initiated in an original format, labeled flexible, and then allowed to solidify and continue without modification. Data gathered from teachers, pupils, and the community by administrators provide insight into current and potential situations which demand modification. Possible changes include 1) regrouping of children, 2) adding faculty and auxiliary personnel, 3) purchasing software and hardware, 4) providing new or extending existing services of the IMC for both the teacher and pupils, 5) changing of emphasis in curriculum content and resultant applied method, 6) adding a public relations program, 7) alerting the professional faculty to the needs of special groups and other atypical children, 8) considering educational requests from the general community for adult and continuing education, and 9) planning physical plant facilities and transportation. At least all nine items have to be considered by educational planners. It is imparative that a systematic on-going evaluation be conducted to periodically modify educational programs which will then continue to reflect the continuity of public concern.

Evaluation: Total Community Involvement

Evaluation of education programming has usually been undertaken by the professional faculty alone. However, because insight to total programming should be complete, all those affected should be given an opportunity to participate in the evaluation. Therefore, the administration should try to involve the faculty, auxiliary staff, pupils, and members of the lay community in the evaluation of educational programs at the local level; even though all of these participants cannot participate equally or have equal voice when their contributions to the evaluation are analyzed for decision making.

Several devices have already been mentioned which provide data for evaluating educational programs. All these devices[18] lend themselves to use by all elements of the educational community; however, response from the learner and the lay community are usually the last included. Opinion questionnaires and interviews have proven successful with children and the lay community. Random sampling techniques are used to select those to be interviewed. These two devices should be included when obtaining data for evaluation because each represents a means by which both the educational product and supporters of educational programs can convey their judgments. When the curriculum reflects concerns of parents and the general public and when the children perceive relevance in their learning experiences, all those affected by educational programs will register their votes of confidence.

Administrative personnel who are possessive and defensive about their educational programs or who try to disguise and withhold information reap increased criticism. Likewise, innovative programs that are initiated arbitrarily without the consent and orientation of those involved are relegated immediately to meager success and subsequent poor evaluation because all elements concerned were not involved in the initial planning. A parallel observation is in order—an effective school public relations program may be the result of an affirmative evaluation of total programming by faculty, auxiliary staff, pupils, and the general community. An informed community that comprehends education issues and problems follows through with unbiased evaluation. Therefore, by involving these groups in the evaluation process, the follow-through of the school public relations program is observable to all those affected by local education programs.

Effect on Individualization of Instruction

Systematic evaluation and modification of an innovative curriculum lends support to the concept of individualized instruction. Multilevel evaluation provides rapid diagnosis of good and bad results so that de-

---

[18] Suggested activities previously noted include 1) paper tests, 2) conference analysis, 3) report cards, 4) parent-teacher conferences, 5) sociometric analysis, 6) interest and attitude inventories, 7) skill check lists, and 8) increased use of area specialists.

veloping learning experiences for individuals can be a reality. The avalanche of data to be evaluated poses a continual challenge for an educational team by demanding modification of the curriculum.

The instructional team should emphasize curriculum design for the individual within the whole class, in a small group, and as an independent learner. Short– and long–term objectives coupled with appropriate evaluation devices now liberate an individual to perceive, behave as, and become that which he is capable of being through the format of individualized personal instruction. Once the learner perceives the vastness of knowledge which he can explore, learning can become an insatiable quest. This realization can result from a single teacher or instructional team which efficiently coordinates the decentralized learning environment and guides the child.

In the final analysis, individual leadership exhibited in the professional behavior of administrators, teachers, auxiliary personnel, and the general community should emerge to allow local school education planners to design programs of study for individuals. When instructional teams and the community consistently work as one, the climate for individualizing instruction is enhanced. Likewise, planning living-learning experiences for the individual learner promotes self-acceptance and worthiness. The child should begin and continue to learn with self-confidence and a genuine feeling of value. Individualized instruction can educate on a mass scale economically and advance the American culture ever onward toward excellence. As John Mason Brown wrote, "Existence is a strange bargain. Life owes us little; we owe it everything. The only true happiness comes from squandering ourselves for a purpose." So it is with individualized instruction—what better way to spend a professional career than in the pursuit of the ideal within one's own lifetime.

SUMMARY

Leadership, the capacity to make decisions and implement them in a workable format, presents itself as a never-ending challenge to professional educators. However, the act of leadership is a shared responsibility among teachers, auxiliary personnel, pupils, and community residents coordinated by the local school administration and boards of education. Insightful leaders function as agents for gathering of data, which in turn serve as guidelines for decision making in terms of short– and long–term local educational objectives. These objectives, which should be in consonance with present local community concerns, should be publicized with a continuous program which uses a multimedia approach to informing the whole community about the realistic status of present and future educational programming.

Leadership should address itself to creating an environment conducive to an effective teaching/learning situation. Elements to be considered are 1) competent teaching, 2) reasonable class size, 3) adequate instructional materials—both software and hardware, 4) enlightened supervision, and 5) boards of education that are leadership-oriented. Coordination of this effort provides a climate in which individualized personal instruction supervised by an instructional team can effectively educate on a mass scale.

Major Themes

1. The school of tomorrow will use instructional technology where curriculum will be designed for an individual child.

2. The neighborhood school will give way to an educational complex of which the elementary school is but one part, consisting of learning zones to meet the demands of an entire community 24 hours a day.

3. The school of tomorrow—regardless of its incorporated innovations in technology, curricula, and personnel management for instruction and unique physical structure—will ultimately be judged by how effective the children's learning experiences are in relation to the educational objectives of the local school district.

4. The instructional team approach to learning experiences makes it possible for increased personalized learning.

5. Flexible modular scheduling provides a means to resolve time allotments when designing educational experiences in an individualized instructional format.

6. As living-learning experiences become increasingly individual-oriented, evaluation becomes more objective.

7. A continuous school public relations program serves as a means for developing an intelligent understanding of the total school operation with respect to a need for change and suggested ways whereby proposed educational programs can be accomplished.

8. School public relations programs have often relied on a narrow base of media; varied media can reach out to inform an increasing number of people in any local community.

9. The reward of a meaningful school public relations program is consistent public pride in and support of the local school's educational programs.

10. All aspects of evaluation should be in terms of short– and long–term objectives established at the local level.

11. Those who attempt to evaluate a child's performance should be concerned with judiciously selecting appropriate evaluative devices for each learning experience.

12. Evaluation of educational offerings is an activity which ought to include the responses of faculty, auxiliary personnel, the learners, and community residents coordinated by local administrators and the board of education.

13. Thorough evaluation of total innovative programming lends support to individualized instruction and provides a basis to educate on a mass scale in the quest for excellence.

SUPPLEMENTARY READINGS

"Accountability Method Makes Failure the Teacher's Fault," *College and University Business*, Vol. 49 (July, 1970), pp. 45ff.

Champlain, Nathaniel L., "Attacks Upon Public Education: Their Significance for Philosophy of Education," *Educational Theory* (July, 1958), pp. 157–61.

Crosby, Muriel, *An Adventure in Human Relations* (Chicago: Follett Publishing Company, 1965).

Dawson, J. E., "New Approaches to Decision Making: Implications for the Elementary School Principal," *National Elementary Principal*, Vol. 47 (May, 1968), pp. 62–69.

Eurich, Alvin C., "Schools Need More than Money," *The Nation*, Vol. CXXCVI, No. 19 (May 10, 1958), pp. 404–6.

Kelly, S. P., "Know Your Community," *American School Board Journal*, Vol. 155 (May, 1968), pp. 14–15.

Lessinger, L. M., "Accountability and Curriculum Reform," *Education Technology*, Vol. 10 (May, 1970), pp. 56–57.

McNally, Harold J. et. al., *Improving the Quality of Public School Programs* (New York: Columbia University Press, 1960).

Messick, S., "Educational Evaluation as Research for Program Improvement," *Childhood Education*, Vol. 46 (May, 1970), pp. 413–14.

Morse, Arthur D., *Schools of Tomorrow—Today* (New York: Doubleday & Company, Inc., 1960).

National Education Association, Research Division, "Ten Criticisms of Public Education," *NEA Research Bulletin*, (December, 1957), pp. 133–74.

Norton, Scott M., "School–Community Relations: New Issues, New Needs," *Clearing House*, Vol. 44 (May, 1970), pp. 538–40.

Olson, C. O. Jr., "Why Teaching Teams Fail," *Peabody Journal of Education*, Vol. 45 (July, 1967), pp. 15–20.

"Restoring the People's Faith in Schools," *School Management*, Vol. 13 (May, 1969), pp. 43–50ff.

Rice, A. H., "Schools Must Revamp Their Public Relations Programs," *Nations Schools*, Vol. 83 (April, 1969), pp. 14ff.

Schwartz, R. and L. S. Lessinger, "Accountability," *Nations Schools*, Vol. 85 (June, 1970), pp. 31–34.

Schmuck, R. A. et. al., "Improving Organizational Problem Solving in a School Faculty," *Journal of Applied Behavioral Science* (October, 1969), pp. 455–82.

Spindler, George D., "Education in a Transforming Culture," *Harvard Educational Review*, Vol. XXV (1955), pp. 145–56.

Wolff, M., "Educational Park Concept," *Wilson Library Bulletin*, Vol. 42 (October, 1967), pp. 173–75.

Appendix

A

MASTERY OF MINIMALS IN AN INTERRELATED APPROACH

NEED FOR INTERRELATEDNESS

Special attention should be given to the concept of mastered minimals in an interrelated approach to instruction because present curricula offerings tend to accent inclusive coverage. When coverage, rather than assimilation of ideas, concepts, and processes through problem solving and the guidance function, is the primary motivating force, the learner may become confused. An able child may work out his own orientation, but most children who study do so in isolated segments. They seldom comprehend the relationships within their living-learning experiences in and out of school.

GREATER SELECTIVITY REQUIRED

A knowledge explosion has made it impossible to possess expertise in all areas of substansive content. Since many classrooms remain self-contained (some with assistance in physical education, art, and music), the need to select what and how something should be taught is a primary function of the contemporary elementary school teacher. Accepting the premise that the elementary school is essentially a skills development area, selectivity should be extended into the area of activities. All too often, learning experiences are only senseless finger exercises.

When an assignment is required, whenever possible have it involve more than one skill and more than one subject content area. For example, given statistical data concerning oil production of the five leading state producers in the United States, activities could cover the following areas: 1) *Arithmetic:* bar, line, and circle graphs; ratios; fractions; estimation; 2) *Natural Science:* geology—stratigraphy; cracking process; 3) *Social Studies:* economics of refining industry and of associated transportation systems; 4) *Art:* construction of models; murals; 5) *Language Arts:* written statements in arithmetic story problems; researched science experiments; abbreviated research papers utilizing instructional materials center resources; discussion groups; student seminars. In this way, larger blocks of time are utilized and the teacher's role diversifies into teacher presentation and assistance of individuals and small groups.

Teachers' Attitudes

Learning reorganization may call for a change in the basic attitude of a teacher toward the act of instruction. Rather than going from page to page and assignment to assignment, a teacher should be viewing the whole curriculum simultaneously and designing those experiences where the interrelatedness of the subject matter instead of the teacher's interests or academic competency is emphasized. This change of focus may require that the classroom teacher spend more time in program analysis. The continual barrage of activity within the elementary curriculum should be systematically surveyed so that the class may be uncluttered and better taught.

Appendix
B

CONTRACTS—A NARROW
BASED FORMAT

CONTRACT AND SIGNIFICANT CLARIFICATION

As attempts to further individualize instruction at the elementary school level multiply, use of the contract as a vehicle to organize learning for children has increased. Depending upon the school system, the format of the contract may vary; however, it essentially contains six subdivisions giving systematic order to a given set of learning: 1) classification, 2) purpose, 3) performance criterion, 4) evaluative criteria, 5) taxonomy, and 6) resources. This format or modification has served to clarify observable behavioral objectives and the level of acceptable performance.

LIMITATIONS OF MANY CONTRACTS

The language of the contract can serve to act as a barrier to learning. In some cases, a teacher inadvertently writes in teacher language which the child can not comprehend. Thus, caution must be continually observed to select language that can be comprehended by the least able at a given age level.

Keeping in mind that instructional materials centers still are not common in the elementary schools across the nation, learning experiences should emphasize the utilization of hardware and software by the learner. In reviewing many individual contracts, there is a tendency to utilize 1) textbooks, 2) workbooks, 3) ditto materials, 4) library reference (e.g., encyclopedias), and 5) commercial games as sources of information. In other words, the old course of study continues in the new contract format.

Broader Concept of Resource Inventory Needed

When contracts are developed, the teacher must broaden the scope of included resources. Besides the traditional resources, one should include such items as 1) filmstrips, 2) films, 3) records, 4) slides, 5) tapes, 6) fieldtrips, 7) guest speakers, 8) interviews, and 9) business and social agency personnel.

Clarification of Resource Entry

The organization of the contract often breaks down with the resource section because of inadequate information entry, lack of subdivision order, and lack of some type of code which indicates required resources. The remaining entries are then optional for the learner. A resource section organization outline might be:

RESOURCES: (*) Required resources

   I. Pamphlets
  II. Books
 III. Encyclopedias
 IV. Community Resources and Personnel
      A. Guest Speaker
      B. Interview
  V. Fieldtrips
 VI. Audio-visual Aids
      A. Records
      B. Filmstrips
      C. Tapes
      D. Slides
VII. Commercial Games

The suggested outline by groupings does not imply that all heading entries should be used per contract. The asterisk (*) can be used to identify those resources which would be required for a particular learning experience. Utilization of many media should be fundamental to individualization of instruction and an integral part of every contract. To individualize the curriculum, a classroom teacher must be concerned continually with providing resources that exercise minimal competencies to the acceptable level and at the same time, are more than just reading vehicles.

Appendix
C

EVALUATION—A CHOICE FOR EACH CHILD

HIGHER LEVEL OF ACHIEVEMENT REQUIRED

When the concept of mastered minimals is followed in curriculum development and learning rate becomes a built-in aspect of enhanced success on an individual basis, the acceptable level of accomplishment is raised to the 90 and 100 percent level of competence in skills. In a system of individualized instruction, fundamental knowledge and skills are more thoroughly comprehended. (Before, a child could achieve a traditional (C) level and have his work acceptable.) Thus, the learner can undertake advanced study with more independence.

Learning for Knowledge and Self-Improvement

One aspect of a classroom teacher's work is to assist each child to gain insight into his own capabilities (which depend upon ability and interest). Knowing that specific objectives have been determined, and that rate of learning is a factor of success, the learner now knows that he can succeed at a minimal level at least. Given continual guidance and encouragement, an elementary school child can reach higher levels of excellence on required minimal concept-skill levels. This increased competence provides a more adequate base for the learner to branch out from the main stream of minimals to investigate related subjects or study one aspect in depth.

Taxonomy—a Key to Quality Learning

The taxonomy category is a primary key to the learning process and subsequent evaluation. Much of instruction today remains at the knowledge and comprehension level. In order to reach and escalate creative involvement, more learning experiences should be elevated to the application and invention levels. At these higher levels of learning, a student learner can be lead to the threshold of his own mind, regardless of innate ability.

EVALUATIVE CRITERIA

Sample Test

The term *sample test* often appears on an individual contract. The words themselves are identified with paper and pencil examinations. Instead, *evaluative criteria* should be used to suggest that other means of judgment can be utilized in determining the acceptability of a given learning experience.

Skills Area

When learning a skill, where discrete parts and concepts are learned and reinforcement is necessary, a percentage response for acceptable accuracy is appropriate.

Applied Competency When skills are necessary to perform other important tasks, evaluation then may require the child to demonstrate his acquired knowledge in the prescribed manner. Again, paper and pencil tests are the most frequently utilized, thus diminishing success because of a reading difficulty, undeveloped writing skills, or lack of poise under the pressure of group-administered and timed examinations.

Varied Media Used for Evaluation

If a multimedia approach is a primary requisite for the individualization of instruction, then varied media should be acceptable for evaluation purposes. Likewise, evaluation should be individually oriented with the options of small group or multigroup participation. Some methods other than traditional paper and pencil tests are 1) individual or group conferences; 2) preparation of models and/or projects where an evaluative criteria is developed with the children, and they in turn evaluate their peers' work; 3) taped responses; 4) art as a mode of presentation; and 5) role playing and sociodrama techniques with appropriate orientation, follow-up discussion, and demonstration of problem-solving techniques.

These five suggestions are by no means inclusive, but serve to point out the fact that standard teacher evaluation procedure and vehicles rely too heavily on the child's ability to read.

Appendix
D

REPORTING EVALUATIONS

EVALUATION—A CONTINUAL CONCERN

In attempting to convey achievement to both the learner and his parents, percentile and letter symbols have traditionally been used by the classroom teacher. Likewise, standardized test achievement scores continue to influence the determination of whether an individual child will pass or fail. Evaluation procedures are still administered to large groups and are timed. For some students, the fear of not succeeding is overwhelming. The concept of grades should be examined more closely. At least one child remarked, "Report cards are for my mother and her friends to compare." An undue emphasis on grade achievement may create a desire for good grades, rather than for acquisition of knowledge and its mastery. We who instruct, regardless of the age level, should address ourselves to the question of whether or not undue stress on grade achievement has undermined the learning process.

Traditional Report Card and Practice

A traditional report card records a numerical and/or letter symbol reflecting level of achievement. At best, this recorded symbol may be an average. It does state in specific terms what a given child, at some time, was or was not able to comprehend and/or apply, in relation to minimal expectations for a given age level. In addition, the traditional report card usually has been accompanied by check lists relative to behavior and/or study habits using a system such as E–S–U or Acceptable—Needs to Improve. Space for parent and/or teacher comment complemented the total report card. Traditional report cards have been distributed at intervals of nine or ten weeks. Thus, except for daily papers and infrequent conferences, significant change may go unreported. Because conferences take time to prepare for, they have tended toward being social gatherings rather than organized professional meetings. Lock-step distribution of report cards precipitated the need for manageable data, and the percentile–letter equivalents have long been an acceptable mode of reporting.

Letter–Conference Practice

Upon diagnosis of educational problems or observable achievement, a classroom teacher should prepare a letter for the parent reporting significant data. This letter need not be lengthy; it should be well organized and written with precise language and brevity. (See pp. 114-17.)

Functional rules for any teacher to follow might be: 1) Begin your letter with an overview statement. 2) In the next paragraph or two, describe the academic and social change in specific terms, including what the school personnel are doing and anticipate doing about the situation. 3) Conclude with a statement eliciting parent cooperation and inviting them for a conference or requesting one when further explanation is desirable. Emphasis should be placed upon the need to call the principal's office and arrange for an appointment.

The parent–teacher conference should follow the format outlined for letter organization. In addition, sample data which specifically illustrate the described situations should be organized and made available for the conference. These data may include cumulative records, daily work samples, anecdotal records, and evaluation statements of other professionally involved personnel, both at the school and at supporting agencies in the community.

In order to maximize effort, insure subsequent quality evaluation, and maintain a high level of empathy, letters and conferences should be dispensed and held in consonance with appropriate need. The following two guidelines may be helpful. 1) By an agreed date, each parent will have received a minimum of one written communication and attended one conference. 2) All communication should be submitted in writing to the building principal to edit. This allows him the opportunity to be informed continually so that appropriate support can be rendered. He can also point out technical omissions which can creep into the work of anyone intimately associated with a given situation. A stenographic assistant for the faculty may be provided. The confidential nature of reporting should be emphasized so that the stenographic assistants do not discuss pupil change with other persons.

Adopting a letter–conference approach to pupil evaluation is an exacting personal experience. Specific details of change rather than subjective composite symbols, which do not provide specific insight into the competency level and nature of the academic or social change, should be stressed.

Instead of using the symbols of the past, including standardized test scores, to provide an accurate measure of pupil change, these evaluative data should be used to diagnose and subsequently create or adjust programs to better meet individual learning capabilities. With traditional evaluations, the specific of competency remains unknown. At best, these markings provided learners and their parents with an awareness of acceptable progress as determined by a given classroom teacher. With a letter–conference approach to reporting pupil change, the accent on individualization and personalizing learning is continued to its logical conclusion in the act of evaluation.

SAMPLE #1: AGE SIX—
SLOW LEARNING DIFFICULTIES (SLD)

This letter could be issued at the beginning of the school year, approximately September 15th.

September 15, 19—

Dear Mr. and Mrs. Clarke:

Because of the information received from the professional folder concerning Jim's difficult adjustment and lack of success in the readiness programs at the kindergarten level, he has been given special tests for the purpose of diagnosing his difficulty in order that a program of study can be designed just for him.

Even though there are apparent learning difficulties, Jim has several friends and he is able to work independently as well as be a part of group activities such as art, music, and physical education.

Jim has reached less than acceptable levels of achievement in those subject areas where he must read. A physical examination by our school physician detected a need for corrective lens which should assist him in being able to focus correctly. The reading specialist works with Jim each day and his assignments have been adjusted in order that he can succeed. At first, progress may be slow; however, by the close of the school year, it is expected that he will be progressing at a normal level expected of a six year old.

For a detailed analysis and description of the specific program designed for Jim, would you meet with me in conference at your earliest convenience. Appointments can be made during the evening hours on Wednesdays as well as before and after school. Telephone 349-4111, Ext. 13.

Sincerely yours,

(Mrs.) Jane W. Snyder
Primary—Level One

SAMPLE #2: AGE NINE—
SELF-MOTIVATED, RAPID LEARNER

This letter could be issued at mid-year, January 15th.

January 15, ——

Dear Mr. and Mrs. Bauer:

At the conclusion of the first term, Allan remains socially adjusted to and among his peers. He is a likeable child who is often sought as a working partner and playmate.

Allan's academic achievements currently are at a level which would normally be expected of a twelve year old in the following areas: vocabulary development, reading comprehension, arithmetic computation and problem solving, and general science knowledge.

You will note decided improvement in his ability to express himself in writing since the beginning weeks of school. His newly found skill of library research has been transferred into report preparation. This is an activity which has been most rewarding to him personally. (See attached report—"Alaskan Seals".)

As a rapid learner, Allan is being encouraged to participate more actively in independent study relative to the enrichment programs for his ability level in such areas as arithmetic and general science.

For additional specific detail concerning Allan's academic and social progress, you are urged to arrange for a conference at your earliest convenience. Call 398-5112, Ext. 27. Conferences can be held on Tuesday evenings as well as before and after school.

Sincerely yours,

D. Craig Walsh
Elementary Level Four

SAMPLE #3: AGE TWELVE—
CULTURALLY DEPRIVED—INNER CITY

This letter could be issued at the end of the school year, June 1st.

Dear Mrs. Johnson:

Since our last conference concerning Alice's behavior and attitude toward school and her classmates, there has been observable improvement. *First*, tardiness is infrequent. *Second*, she no longer starts fights with other children. *Third*, there has been minimal improvement in her school work. As we agreed, there was a need for more parental concern to be shown, and your efforts have transferred to her work at school.

Because of her marked success during the last quarter of the school year, the elementary school counselor and I believe that Alice would profit by going on to the next level, even though she has not achieved acceptable success in all areas of her studies.

Alice's achievement record and work samples will be forwarded to her counselor in order that a correct course of study can be designed for her beginning next fall.

So that you understand Alice's strengths and limitations, both academic and social, Mr. Donaldson, Elementary School Counselor, and I would like to meet with you at your earliest convenience to discuss Alice's total past and proposed school program. For your convenience, conferences can be scheduled before school, after school, and Wednesday evenings. Call 445-7737, Ext. 37.

Sincerely yours,

Erma J. Peterson
Elementary—Level Six
Glenn P. Donaldson
Elementary School Counselor

Appendix

E

CASE STUDIES: GUIDANCE FUNCTION APPLIED*

CASE #1—ROSALEE

Rosalee, a robust five year old, hit kindergarten with an explosive effect. She was energetic, bright, and mean to her classmates. The kindergarten teacher observed Rosalee's acclimation to the kindergarten setting; and, after a series of observations, she was prepared with data to present to the principal. The principal had little time to become deeply involved with the case because of his administrative duties. Parent conferences were held in order to obtain background information about Rosalee. The parents interpreted Rosalee's behavior from two points of view. To her father, Rosalee was a normal girl with an outgoing personality. He commented that he liked outgoing girls, those who were not meek and timid. In contrast, Rosalee's mother felt that she was not a normal child; she was searching for insights on how to understand and live with her.

The kindergarten year came to a close. Rosalee was promoted to the next level in the primary school. Her cumulative record described excellent progress. The kindergarten teacher evaluated her as bright, but a discipline problem.

When Rosalee was in the primary school, she made very rapid progress in the beginning of her formalized reading program. During the summer recess, she had acquired some reading skills on her own initiative. After two months of school, Rosalee began to show signs of developing unac-

* The case study data for this text was provided by Dr. Marie O. McNeff, Assistant Professor of Education, Augsburg College, Minneapolis, Minnesota.

ceptable work habits and not completing assigned work. Her work was characterized by being consistently incomplete.

As a result of this observable behavior, the teacher made an appointment with the principal to discuss Rosalee's problems. Parent-teacher conferences were held. Again, Rosalee's father was quite proud of how his daughter could physically maneuver any child in the block. Her mother, however, wanted and asked for help. The father left the conference with the attitude that the classroom teacher just wasn't appreciative of Rosalee's tremendous potential; the mother went away feeling quite frustrated, thinking, "Is there nothing we can do to help Rosalee?"

The first year in the primary school ended. Although all mental ability tests indicated Rosalee had potential for completing the primary school in two years, she was placed with a group of pupils who might need four years to complete the primary school. Rosalee entered school in the fall term of the following year, armed with energy to expand the four walls of any classroom . . . and she did. Near the close of October, Rosalee was again brought to the attention of the principal by her classroom teacher.

And so, on and on, the vicious circle of problem identification became the pattern of Rosalee's school life. Each year she was identified as having a problem, and each year her cumulative folder became thicker and thicker. No program of specific help was ever formulated for follow through to assist this child. This is obviously a case where guidance at the elementary school level was badly needed.

CASE #2—MRS. JACKSON'S FIFTH GRADE CLASS

Mrs. Jackson, fifth grade teacher at Greenwood Elementary School, looked over her class list and plans, remembering the many activities that had transpired during the day. She had worked with this group of students for a period of about six weeks. During this time, she had had the opportunity to get to know the students on an individual basis.

For instance, look at Martin. Martin and his mother appeared in the Greenwood Elementary School Office in mid-September. Martin was a new enrollee for the school year, having moved into the district from a city approximately 100 miles away. During the initial visit with the principal, Martin's mother indicated that the previous school teacher had advised them to retain Martin another year in fifth grade.

At the beginning of the present school year, Martin had been assigned to a sixth grade level, but the required school work had proven extremely difficult for him. Roland, Martin's older brother, was very successful as a student, according to the mother's report; and Martin felt sibling pressure due to his academic slowness. Pressure was being exerted not only by his brother, but also from relatives, especially grand-parents and aunts. After further discussion, it was decided that Martin would be assigned to Mrs. Jackson's classroom.

As Mrs. Jackson observed Martin, she noticed that he was quick to complete his work so that he could say he was the first one to finish, even though the quality was less than acceptable. As Mrs. Jackson made herself available for individual help, Martin would conceal his work, almost indicating that he was ashamed to have anyone observe it. This was one of the first items to concentrate on—helping Martin to feel that he had worthwhile contributions to make and to improve his own self-concept. Mrs. Jackson had made a note to have a conference with Mr. Rose, the elementary counselor, for some suggestions on how she could incorporate activities into the classroom that would improve Martin's self-concept.

Next Mrs. Jackson's attention was turned to Rex. Rex's mother had stopped by the classroom during the first week of school and requested aid in working with her son. At home, Rex displayed a violent temper which was almost uncontrollable. Mrs. Jackson had never seen this dis-play of temper at school, but she did contact the guidance counselor. After several conferences with Rex and his parents, Mr. Rose referred them to the Community Child Welfare Agency for further help.

Rex was a child who needed much more intensive and specialized care than the staff at Greenwood School was qualified to provide. Through the agency's liasion officer, Mr. Rose was able to keep Mrs. Jackson informed and involved with the specialized program for Rex. Coopera-tive planning among the parents, the school faculty, and Child Welfare Agency personnel was possible through the efforts of Mr. Rose. He became the central coordinator through which all the people who were working with Rex were communicating.

Then there was Sally and her clique of three girl friends. These girls were in different classrooms within the school. If Sally or one of her friends wasn't pregnant before they left elementary school, it wouldn't be because they weren't trying. Boy–girl relations was the major con-cern of these girls. Mrs. Jackson had met with Mr. Rose concerning the girls. Mr. Rose had involved the four girls in a group counseling situa-tion, in addition to individual counseling sessions.

Actually, Mr. Rose was able to identify most of the children. Two of them had suffered school phobia at the kindergarten level. Now they were so completely involved in school that no indication of previous problems was visible. One child hadn't communicated verbally for a period of six months. Now it was difficult to get him to let others speak because he feels he has something to contribute. As an elementary school counselor, Mr. Rose's contribution to the children's academic and social growth at Greenwood Elementary School far exceeds his salary. Mrs. Jackson's last thought, before looking at arithmetic papers on her desk, was, "What did we ever do before we had elementary school counselors?"

CASE #3—SUSAN

Mrs. R., Susan's *classroom teacher*, noted that Susan appeared very nervous in the classroom setting. She was unable to sit still for any length of time. Susan continually popped out of her desk chair or jumped around the room. On occasion, she would resort to lying on the floor. Every time Susan came to the teacher's desk, she picked up some object and stood there fingering it in silence. One afternoon, she went to the restroom and continued flushing the toilets until they overflowed. During an art lesson, she ruined a Christmas decoration she was making. Her hand coordination appeared to be very poor. Following this incident, Susan took paper and painted layer on layer of paint until there was only a limp wet piece of paper inundated with a mixture of paint. During one noon break, she deliberately kicked down two snowmen that some other children had built. Upon hearing this report, she violently beat on her head with her fists. Academically, Susan was working below the third grade level.

The *school psychologist* reported that, according to the results from the Stanford Binet, Susan had an I. Q. score of 106. On the Otis group test, she received a rating of 101. These test results indicated that Susan was within the average range of intelligence. During the testing situation, it appeared that Susan had more difficulty with the output than the input side of performance. She had difficulty in utilizing her perceptions in a meaningful way. Susan earned a perceptual quotient that would place her in the lower 2 percent of the total population for her age. This was lower than would have been anticipated for her general ability. It is evident that the low perceptual quotient has had implications for all school activities—particularly reading and arithmetic.

Mrs. S., the *school nurse*, had contacted Susan's parents three times during the present school year to encourage them to take Susan to a medical doctor for a physical examination. On each occasion, Susan's mother indicated that she would try to get an appointment, and she always had an excuse to explain why she hadn't been able to keep a previously scheduled appointment. Mrs. S. had remarked that it appeared to her that it was an example of uncooperative parents.

Mr. R., *the school social worker*, had contacted Susan's parents and arranged for a home visitation. During the home visitation, her father revealed that he had muscular dystrophy, a hereditary disease characterized by progressive muscle atrophy. He was very concerned about his children because the disease may have been transmitted to them. Susan's father was afraid to take his children to the doctor for fear of the report. Both Susan's parents wanted the best for each of their children. Susan's mother could not understand why Susan wasn't maintaining satisfactory progress at school. She stated that Susan did not have any problem last year. Later on during the visit, she indicated that Susan had not wanted to go to school last year, and would try to find excuses so that she would not have to attend. Both Susan and her brother were overprotected by their parents.

On several occasions, Susan appeared in the *principal's* office for disciplinary action. When Susan became disruptive within the classroom, she was sent to the principal's office. At times she just sat in the office. When the principal was able to see Susan, they discussed her behavior. Susan always appeared to be sorry for her actions, and promised to try harder the next time. She expressed a real liking for her classroom teacher.

Susan visited the *speech therapist* three times a week for a twenty minute period. She was in a group with two other children. During the speech therapy sessions, she was always cooperative and enjoyed her work with the therapist. She was always on time, and appeared reluctant to leave at the conclusion of each session. Susan was improving in speech, to the extent that it was anticipated that she would be dismissed in about two months.

Problem Identification

Susan has been described by six members on the professional staff at school. The elementary school counselor would add more information about Susan. Hopefully, through the efforts of the elementary counselor, a more complete person will be revealed, and a more definite plan of action will be initiated for Susan's benefit. Additional information about Susan is available in her cumulative record file. The use of such information is crucial at this point, or its compilation is useless. Without the services of an elementary school counselor, Susan would be caught in a vicious circle of problem identification. Through the services of the elementary counselor, that circle can be broken, with the result being help for Susan. No rapid, magical solutions to the complexity of her problems will be released through the elementary counselor, but there will be a decrease in the spinning of wheels in the endless circle of problem identification.

Functional Role of the Elementary School Counselor

In this particular case, the elementary counselor would begin by making plans to observe Susan in many varied situations in the school. He would arrange for staffing so that all people working with Susan could participate in case conference sessions in order to share their findings. Within these sessions, the sharing of information would be a prelude to specific recommendations for staffing and program aid. The elementary counselor would be responsible for the initiation and follow-through of the staff's rcommendations. Specific materials would be obtained or developed through the efforts of the elementary counselor, so that a problem such as perceptual difficulty, which was noted by the psychologist, could be decreased or eliminated. Recommendations offered by the various professional personnel would be translated into workable activities for Susan that would be directed by the elementary school counselor in cooperation with the instructional team.

The classroom teacher is of primary importance to the success of Susan's prescribed program. Once the recommendations have been translated by the elementary school counselor, the teacher is in a position to implement the activities. If the program is to be initiated within the classroom, Susan's teacher must be involved in the initial planning and all phases of staffing and program analysis.

At the time of staffing, it may be decided that the counselor should undertake individual counseling with Susan, for the purpose of forming a more positive attitude about herself and the school. The remedial reading teacher may be brought into the case. Tutorial services, available through the Pupil Personnel Services Department, may be requested so that Susan might function closer to her reported intellectual capacity. Parental involvement, through the efforts of the social worker, would be continued. Follow-through and feedback of initiated programs are fundamental for on-going analysis so that the program can be modified. Because some initiated programs may not work with Susan, it is necessary to have feedback to assist the professional staff to make decisions to discontinue or replace existing phases of the prescribed program.

Conclusion

Not all of Susan's problems will be solved. It is the purpose of the elementary guidance program to help Susan to become independently responsible. Through an elementary guidance program, potential problems may be prevented. Identified problems can be coped with before they are so deep-seated that they can never be cured.

Appendix
F

GUIDANCE OF INDEPENDENT LEARNING EXPERIENCES

EMERGENCE OF INDEPENDENT
LEARNING EXPERIENCES

Until recently, all children in a classroom usually participated in identical learning experiences. However, children were encouraged to work independently and on independent interest projects in addition to their regular assigned work. This independent study was not considered a part of the regular curriculum for elementary school children. Today, industry has provided children with books, games, toys, and other educational equipment whereby an insatiable curiosity may have been whetted even before a child's entry into the elementary school. Thus, independent study is an acceptable mode of learning for many children, beginning at the primary levels of learning.

GUIDING INDEPENDENT LEARNING EXPERIENCES

Perceiving independent study as an integral part of the elementary curriculum is necessary for every elementary school teacher. During these formative years, any child may be provided with the needed assistance which is the foundation of a life-long career. Although specific orientations may change, curiosity is sustained over time. Hence, teacher sensitivity to the socio-dynamics within a classroom, individual interests, and available resources, used with effective management practice, provides a flexible framework for guiding a child or group of children in independent learning experiences.

Ways of Diagnosing

The periodic administration of simple sociograms may provide insight into the social structure of any given group of children. Of particular interest to a teacher are: 1) mutual choices, 2) apparent cliques established/or developing, 3) the outstanding child or children as chosen by the peer group, and 4) the isolate. Keep in mind that the social complexion of the class will change depending upon the nature of the questions asked of the children.

Administering an interest inventory every month or so provides a teacher with information concerning the changing interests of the children. The teacher should make an item analysis of each interest so as to find out which children have mutual interests for the purpose of both individual and group study or for possible contributions to the class as a whole. An additional help is to compare mutual interests with mutual choices from the sociogram data. Often these data coincide.

Based upon these means of diagnosis, team planning and teaching—buttressed by the resources of the instructional materials center—provide both additional professional guidance and materials with which to extend the learner's horizons of knowledge. Pupil–teacher planning is a fundamental aspect of successful independent study guidance. Pupil involvement is a catalytic agent which induces self-motivation and subsequent levels of excellence in living-learning independent study.

GLOSSARY

Ability grouping Homogeneous grouping.

Adult and continuing education programs Short-term courses in adult interest areas such as weaving, wood working, china painting, Great Books, nutrition, filing income tax forms, and budgeting, as well as formal study programs.

Auxiliary assistants Lay people who provide clerical help and supervise cafeterias and playgrounds, relieving teachers from non-instructional duties. Auxiliary personnel do not make professional decisions.

Behavioral objectives Statements of observable behavior competency which include identified competency and level of acceptable performance. For example, "Each student leaving the elementary school shall be able to comprehend and successfully apply the processes approach to the analysis of scientific principles, such as '*Magnetism:* LIKE poles repel and UNLIKE poles attract.' "

Case conference A meeting for the assimilation of diagnostic data prepared by lay and professional personnel to evaluate pupil change and make subsequent recommendations for action. The group of resource persons is usually coordinated by the building principal.

Committee work A form of classroom organization consisting of small groups of children working within well defined limits on an assigned project with a predetermined outcome.

Community agencies Both personnel and services that may be significant to curriculum development and solution of problems of individuals or groups of children. Some of these agencies are social welfare agencies, mental health clinics, and all industry.

Differential grouping A situation in which a classroom teacher analyzes living-learning experiences and appropriately selects which children will study independently, as a group, or as a whole class and at what times the groupings shall be in effect. This type of grouping is used to implement pupil-teacher planning and the guidance function.

Differential learning   The common situation in which there are children with varied abilities in a given classroom. Thus, an effective teacher is duty-bound to create living-learning situations in several formats in order that each child under his supervision can achieve success.

Evaluation   Both formal and informal methods of appraising on-going programs for the purpose of making decision on modification, continuance, and deletion of aspects of the programs.

Exceptional children   Those who are mentally retarded, cerebral palsied, physically handicapped, blind, or bright and gifted.

Heterogeneous grouping   An attempt by a principal to standardize each section of a grade level by assigning a cross section of pupils with different learning abilities and recognizable special problems to each classroom.

Homogeneous grouping   An attempt by a principal to reduce the instructional range within a classroom. Criteria for pupil assignments are usually a combination of intelligence quotient and reading level. This type of grouping in the elementary school has been associated more frequently with the rapid learner only than with the entire span of elementary school pupils.

Independent learning, full cycle   A program involving all of these learning components: self-motivation, identification of problems to be solved, systems analysis, conclusion, and extension of acquired knowledge in technological or related activities as a follow-up. When a learning environment is used flexibly in conjunction with pupil–teacher planning, the independent learning cycle operates under its own momentum.

Independent study skills   Skills which enable the learner to function independently in small group and whole class situations. They include self-control; efficient use of time; operational knowledge of audio-visual equipment; comprehension of written material; ability to organize and record data; ability to make hypotheses, comparisons, contrasts, and summaries; and ability to draw conclusions.

Individualized instruction   That mix of classroom organizations for learning used in consonance with innovation to allow a pupil to become increasingly more independent of the teachers and more dependent upon his own resources in the learning process.

Ingraded classroom   A nongraded classroom in a self-contained or semi-departmentalized school organization in which the pupil's personalized program of study is not continually adjusted to his readiness level once performance criteria have been achieved.

Inquiry-involvement A classroom method, associated with a flexible child-centered curriculum where students share the responsibility for curriculum decisions with the classroom teacher whenever possible.

Instructional materials center That area of the school which houses the library and audio-visual facilities and functions as a learning center for both teacher and pupil.

Instructional media center Instructional materials center.

Module A block of time from ten to twenty minutes in length.

Module system A school organization plan in which the day is divided into modules for instruction which are requested in advance by teachers. Each child is usually scheduled for a minimum of 60 percent of his time. The remaining time is utilized in independent study and special assistance. Schedules may change daily or weekly, depending upon available administrative staff and computer technology.

Multigraded classroom A class with a range of two or three chronological years, allowing a child to work and play in a peer group similar to that of his own neighborhood.

Nongraded classroom A school organization plan which removes grade levels, eliminating group competition to allow the child to move at his own pace and set his own standards with the supervision of the teacher.

Paraprofessionals Classroom auxiliary personnel.

Programmed learning A sequential skill study which is followed by the pupil without the assistance of classroom teachers. After a predetermined comprehension score has been established, the pupil progresses at his own rate from step to step and level to level toward specified goals.

Self-contained classroom One in which all curriculum decision making is the professional responsibility of one teacher who more often than not is a specialist in reading. Simultaneously, this same teacher must be competent in a wide range of academic knowledge and possess the know-how of lateral transmission in order to create effective learning experiences for individual, small group, and whole class groups. This type of class is usually graded.

Semi-departmentalization A system in which students stay with a core teacher for a half-day and with subject area specialists for the rest of the day.

Small towns Those settlements with a population of 2500 or less (as defined by the U.S. Bureau of the Census).

Supplementary personnel Those persons and agencies that assist a classroom teacher in carrying out his professional responsibility in the education of an assigned group of children.

Team learning A type of classroom organization in which small groups of children (from two to six members) combine their talents in the inquiry–discovery approach to learning with minimal direction from the teacher.

Team teaching A type of instructional organization in which two or more teachers are given responsibility working together for all or significant parts of the instruction of one group of students which is assigned to them (as defined by Shaplin and Olds).

Telling-lecture A classroom method, traditionally associated with the graded classroom and a teacher-centered curriculum, in which the teacher explains facts to passive students.

Traditional failure The "learning-to-forget" practiced by pupils in many graded organizational units. It is a situation where the letter or percentile grade reigns, the tests relate to immediate recall, and learning ability is only a secondary factor in evaluation. In this situation, adjustment in learning experiences seldom takes place.

Index